Tony Morris is a book publisher, dedicated walker and former board director of Theatre de Complicite. He grew up in Belfast, studied at Cambridge and now lives in London with his wife and their young daughter. He first encountered Buddhism fifteen years ago. His writings include *In the Footsteps of the Buddha* and *How Buddhism Came to Oxford*.

The Lotus flower is often used as a Buddhist symbol. The deeper the mud in which it grows the more lustrously it blooms, a metaphor for the way we can transform the dirt and difficulties of life to create value and beauty. The so-called Lotus Sutra is widely regarded as one of the Buddha's most profound teachings.

SERIES EDITOR: TONY MORRIS

Available now

What Do Christians Believe? Malcolm Guite
What Do Druids Believe? Philip Carr-Gomm
What Do Muslims Believe? Ziauddin Sardar

Published in Autumn 2006

What Do Astrologers Believe? Nicholas Campion
What Do Greens Believe? Joseph Smith
What Do Existentialists Believe? Richard Appignanesi
What Do Jews Believe? Edward Kessler

Forthcoming

What Do Hindus Believe? Rachel Dwyer
What Do Pagans Believe? Graham Harvey
What Do Zionists Believe? Colin Shindler

What Do **BUDDHISTS** Believe?

Tony Morris

Granta Books

London

Granta Publications, 2/3 Hanover Yard, Noel Road, London N1 8BE
First published in Great Britain by Granta Books 2006

A CIP catalogue record for this book is available
from the British Library.

ISBN-10: 1-86207-835-1
ISBN-13: 978-1-86207-835-2

3 5 7 9 10 8 6 4 2

Typeset by M Rules
Printed in the UK by CPI Bookmarque, Croydon, CR0 4TD

*This book is dedicated
with my deepest respect and gratitude
to the Buddhists of
Polstead Road, Vicarage Road, Albert Street
and
above all
Courthope Road*

Contents

Acknowledgements

Various friends and scholars have offered advice and comment throughout this book's gestation: Eddy Canfor-Dumas, Dr Rachel Dwyer, Professor Richard Gombrich, Sara Hagel, Dr Elizabeth Harris, Professor Peter Harvey, Kenneth Jones, Jo Lane, Sarah Norman, Jim Pym, Fiona Riches, Dr Helen Waterhouse, Dr Gay Watson and, above all, Professor Damien Keown, whose knowledge and expertise illuminate every page. I salute them for being so generous and helpful. I also hasten to add that they all disagreed with some of my emphases – and also with each others! Buddhism is reassuringly unmonolithic.

No one could have had better publishers than George Miller, Sajidah Ahmad, Bella Shand and Sarah Wasley at Granta Books.

To all of the above I express my deepest thanks.

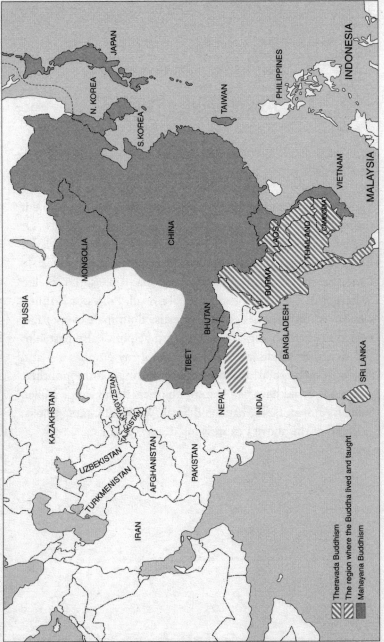

Buddhism in Asia

Theravada Buddhism

The region where the Buddha lived and taught

Mahayana Buddhism

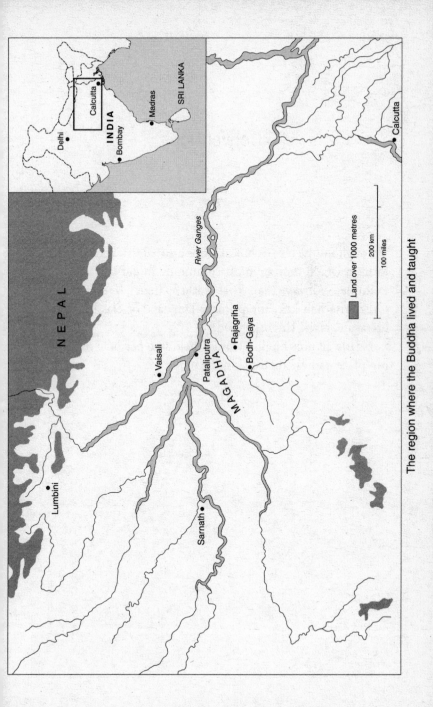

The region where the Buddha lived and taught

Conventions

Throughout the text technical terms are mainly expressed in the form in which they are most commonly found in English: for example, *Karma* (Sanskrit) rather than *Kamma* (Pali). Otherwise Sanskrit, the primary language of classical Indian literature, is the language used.

Nearly all non-English words (including personal names but not place names) are listed in the index.

Preface

Buddhism is one of the world's oldest and most widespread religions with a history spanning some 2,500 years. It has over four hundred million adherents and there are Buddhists today in almost every country in the world. How can one possibly attempt to bring all that diversity within the compass of a hundred or so small pages?

I can't. What I *can* do is try to give a sense of some of the most important and interesting facets of Buddhism and some of the reasons why, in an age which seems increasingly disenchanted with organized religion, Buddhism appears to be thriving.

The teachings of Buddhism are vast and various, and it has a well-developed mystical and philosophical side. At its core, however, is a simple set of propositions and practices. Its emphasis has always been, and remains, how to live a wise, happy, compassionate and fulfilled life.

My hope is that some of the questions I have asked will be the questions you would want to ask, and that this little book will take you a step further on your own journey of discovery.

Tony Morris
July 2005

Chronology

BCE

c.566–486	Traditional dates for the life of the Buddha
c.485–405	Life of the Buddha according to recent research
c.405	The First Council at Rajagriha
c.325	The 'Great Schism'
c.321–184	Mauryan Dynasty
c.268–231	Reign of Ashoka
c.250	Buddhism brought to Sri Lanka by Mahinda
c.25	Pali Canon written down

CE

0	Origins of the Mahayana
c.65	First record of Buddhism in China
c.100	Lotus Sutra
3rd Century	First evidence for Buddhism in Cambodia and Vietnam
4th Century	Buddhism arrives in Korea and Burma
500–600	Development of Tantric Buddhism (Vajrayana)
6th Century	Buddhism arrives in Japan
600–700	First trace of Buddhism in Tibet
1200–1300	Buddhism virtually disappears from India
12th Century	Zen arrives in Japan from China and Korea

1230	First record of Buddhism in Cambodia
13th Century	Buddhism becomes official religion in Thailand
c.1850	Beginning of Western interest in Buddhism
1881	Pali Text Society founded
1907	Buddhist Society of Great Britain and Ireland founded
1950	Invasion of Tibet by China
1959	Dalai Lama flees Tibet
c.1960	Origins of 'Engaged Buddhism'
1987	American Buddhist Congress founded
1989	Dalai Lama awarded Nobel Peace Prize
1995	UK Association of Buddhist Studies founded

1

What does it mean?

Who is a Buddhist?

The Buddha was once asked by an eager student what happens to an enlightened person when they die. He deflected the question with a joke. But the earnest enquirer persisted. So the Buddha turned to him and said:

> Listen – if you had just been shot by a poison-tipped arrow, you wouldn't be standing there asking me, 'Who fired it? What did they look like? Where did they come from?' . . . You'd be saying: 'Help! Get this arrow out! Quick!'[1]

The point the Buddha wanted to make is that it is important to attend to what is urgent and a matter of fact, rather than getting distracted by speculations and theories. We must live in the here and now.

Buddhism is not anti-intellectual. It has a profound and elaborate philosophical dimension, refined over centuries by some of the world's most sophisticated scholars. The provenance of the arrow would be critical to a full and proper investigation of the incident, and the Buddha was not seeking to duck the question. The point he wanted to stress is that we need to call for the doctor first and the forensic scientist second. Priorities matter.

This fundamentally pragmatic approach is what makes Buddhism so distinctive. It is also what makes the title of this book at first appear rather odd. For Buddhists aren't primarily concerned with *believing* and *thinking*; their main interest is in *being* and *doing*. Buddhists do what they do because they want to become wiser and happier. It is hard to think of any religion or philosophy that wouldn't support the same aims, but few are as explicit about it. In the words of the Dalai Lama: 'The very purpose of life is to seek happiness.' What that means in Buddhist practice (as well as theory) is the subject of this book.

There is only one way to find out whether Buddhism works or not: by testing the teachings in daily life. Of course it is important to listen to what other people have to say, and to read and study the scriptures (which are voluminous); but there is no substitute for direct, actual, personal experience.

The Buddha was emphatic about this. 'That which you affirm [must be] that which you have realised, seen, known for yourself.'[2] Every teaching should be tested rigorously before being accepted or rejected. Belief based on theory was one thing, knowledge grounded in personal experience another.

The Buddha might not altogether have approved of the title of this book therefore. Perhaps a better question would be: 'Does Buddhism work? Does it make your life more meaningful?' The answer to this would be a resounding and unequivocal 'Yes'. There aren't many questions to which over four hundred million people, living in all corners of the world, would respond unanimously, so this in itself is highly significant.

And the question gets more interesting the more it is explored. 'Meaningfulness' can be understood on a number of levels:

Philosophically: why are we born?
Historically: how did we get here?
Psychologically: who are we?
Morally: how should we behave?
Politically: what kind of society do we want?
Cosmically: where are we going?

This book attempts to offer some answers to all of these questions, and I hope several more.

Finally, how much has Buddhism changed over time? Is being a Buddhist *now* any different from being a Buddhist in the past? Two hundred years ago there were virtually no Buddhists in the West. Now there are over a million in Europe and approximately three million in the United States. Two millennia ago there were very few Buddhists outside India and hundreds of thousands in it. Now they represent only a tiny minority of that subcontinent's population, whilst elsewhere in the world their numbers are growing rapidly.

The increasing popularity of Buddhism across very different cultures and at a time of increased secularism and suspicion of 'organized religion' is interesting in itself. Why are more and more people in the West taking up Buddhism? What is it that they think it has to offer that other belief systems don't? Is it becoming more popular because it answers some of the pressing questions posed by living in the twenty-first century? Or has the definition of Buddhism become so flexible as to be effectively useless?

It is clear, for example, that people who call themselves Buddhist vote in many different ways (or don't, or aren't allowed to vote), so there can't be such a thing as a monolithic 'Buddhist view' of politics. Similarly, not all Buddhists are vegetarians, or agree about the role of women in society, or the causes of poverty and its alleviation, or the best way to raise children or prevent war. Buddhists even seem to disagree about some apparently very basic 'theological' questions, like which is the most important of the Buddha's teachings, what precisely it means to be enlightened, or whether or not belief in rebirth is essential. Some commentators feel we should talk about 'Buddhisms' in the plural and focus on its practitioners rather than searching for a set of core, universal premises.

So: Who, or what, is a Buddhist? The definition adopted in this book has the merit of being both simple and incontrovertible – which is not to say that everyone would agree on it: a Buddhist is someone who says they are a Buddhist. Buddhism, according to this account at least, is a question of identity, self-consciousness and choice.

How often or how intensely Buddhists ask themselves about their identity will obviously depend on who they are and on their circumstances. To be born into a Buddhist family, in a culture where Buddhists predominate and where its outward signs – temples, statues, robed monks – are everywhere to be seen, is very different from being a first-generation 'convert' in a culture where Buddhists are in a tiny minority. One is the inherited norm, the other an active choice.

Which brings us back to the final, implicit part of the question raised at the beginning: what Buddhists say and do – how people act meaningfully on their beliefs. The two things don't follow necessarily. I often wonder whether, if he were to come back today, the Buddha would recognize many of the things which are being said and done in his name – just as I wonder whether Christ or Muhammad would be horrified by some of the causes for which their support is invoked. There are misguided zealots and hypocrites in all cultures. But it would be interesting to know, at the very least, *why* Buddhists agree that being a Buddhist makes their lives more meaningful and how they feel – or possibly even *believe* – it affects the way they live.

2

Where are the Buddhists?

Mapping the Message

> It is rare to be born a human being. The number of those
> endowed with human life is as small as the amount of earth one
> can place on a fingernail . . . Truly it is more difficult to be born as
> a human being than it is to lower a thread from the heavens above
> and pass it through the eye of a needle at the bottom of the sea.[3]

To be born a Buddhist or to encounter 'the law of the Buddha'
is rarer still, according to tradition – as rare as it would be for 'a
one-eyed turtle to encounter a floating sandalwood log with a
hole in it that fits him exactly'.[4]

Over the centuries, millions of people have succeeded, however – to the extent that Buddhism is the world's fourth biggest
religion.[5] In part this has to do with geography. Buddhism first
evolved in Asia, the world's most populous continent. From its
epicentre in the plains around the River Ganges it travelled west
to Afghanistan, north to Nepal and Tibet, and east, via the silk

route, to China, Korea, Vietnam, Taiwan and Japan. South, Buddhism spread over the sub-continent to Sri Lanka and across the seas to Thailand, Burma, Cambodia and Laos. For two millennia it extended its influence, adapting with great effect to the prevailing conditions of the people and places it touched.

Then, in the nineteenth and twentieth centuries, came mass migration by sea and air. As Asians moved to the new worlds of opportunity they took their religion with them. Buddhism began to extend so far east that it became Western too, stretching across the Pacific and into the Americas. Meanwhile, European explorers and intellectuals travelling in the other direction began to encounter this fascinating strain of oriental thought. Even war and conflict conspired to make the world more aware of Buddhism, the horrors of Japan, China, Vietnam and especially Tibet forcing a mass exodus of Buddhist émigrés. In the world today only Africa and Arabia remain relatively untouched, though even here there are growing pockets of Buddhist adherents.

Censuses of religious affiliation are notoriously imprecise, but the estimates below give some idea of the relative distribution of Buddhists throughout the world:[6]

Africa	85k
Asia	409m
Europe	1.8m
UK	200k
Americas	3.6m
USA	2.9m
Oceania	463k

The evidence further suggests that Buddhism is growing fastest in the West. Buddhism, it would appear, is not only one of the world's oldest religions; it is also, according to some classifications, one of the most popular 'new religious movements'!

In each region of the world Buddhism has its figureheads. The best known in the West are those who feature prominently on the screen and in the press. The actor Richard Gere is a vocal and visible advocate. Orlando Bloom is a recent convert. The Vietnamese monk and pioneer of 'engaged Buddhism', Thich Nhat Hanh, has sold tens of thousands of copies of his books, as have – to name but a few – Sogyal Rinpoche, author of *The Tibetan Book of Living and Dying*, Jack Kornfield, psychotherapist, psychologist and author of *A Path with Heart* and Lama Surya Das, author of *Awakening the Buddha Within*.

Several Buddhists have emerged from musical celebrity – Leonard Cohen, Tina Turner, Herbie Hancock, Sandie Shaw, Philip Glass. Two of the world's greatest footballers, Roberto Baggio and Ronaldo, have also been connected with Buddhism.

In political terms the conspicuous heroism and bravery of Aung San Suu Kyi in opposing the military dictatorship in Burma has earned her international renown and the Nobel Prize for peace. Less familiar on the world political stage but with a devoted (and often large) following in their own countries, are leaders like Daisaku Ikeda (president of the Soka Gakkai organization in Japan), Dr A. T. Ariyaratne (founder of the Sarvodaya Shramadana movement in Sri Lanka), Sulak Sivaraksa (an outspoken social critic in Thailand) and Sangharakshita (founder of Friends of the Western Buddhist Order in the UK).

And of course, smiling benevolently from the cover of a paperback near you, is the world's most famous living Buddhist, the Dalai Lama, Tenzin Gyatso, whose books have sold in their millions and who has inspired so many people to think about the cause of his homeland, Tibet, through his writings, teachings, interviews and, above all, by his indefatigable example of passionate conviction and compassionate dedication.

3

How did we get here?

What Siddhartha Did

I am beyond being,
My knowledge undivided,
My mind unmarked,
All identifying with its objects fallen away.
I have crossed out of craving into freedom
By my own efforts, my own understanding.
I have no teacher,
No equal anywhere,
Alone, Enlightened . . .
I have vanquished the sleep of ignorance.
I am awake,
A Buddha.[7]

Without the Buddha there would be no Buddhism. It is probably worth starting with this statement of the obvious, because it is one of the few assertions on which all Buddhists can agree. In a religion of extraordinary – some would say bewildering – diversity, with no equivalent to a central authority figure or pope, no one agreed official canon, and no effective mechanism for enforcing orthodoxy or punishing 'heresy', it is important at least to have a founder. All Buddhists can trace their spiritual ancestry back to this source, this single individual. Every Buddhist alive today can at least point to him and agree: here is where our story begins.

Then the complications set in. For although we have a name and a starting point, we don't have a firm date, a physical image, a contemporaneous document, or even much archaeology. As one biographer puts it, we would be very hard-pressed to come up with enough 'facts' to fill a single-paragraph entry in *Who's Who*.

We cannot arrive at a 'definitive' account of the Buddha's life any more than Christian scholars have been able to compose a reliable biography of Jesus. What we have instead is a legend, rich in symbolism and allegory – a series of key moments and psychological insights threaded together in a sequence: birth, maturity, renunciation, quest, awakening, liberation, teaching, death.

He was born Siddhartha Gautama (Buddha is an honorific title rather than a name, meaning 'one who is awakened' or 'enlightened'). He grew up in what is now Nepal, in the plains below the Himalayas. And he lived, taught and died in northern India.

He is often referred to as Shakyamuni or 'the Sage of the Shakyas'. The Shakyas were one of a number of peoples spread out along the fertile fringes of the Ganges basin, living in more or less independent groupings or clans. Siddhartha's father, Shuddhodana, was a tribal elder, possibly even a king. As such his baby son would have been born into what were, for the time, very comfortable circumstances.

Some scholars put the date of Siddhartha's birth at 563 BCE, others claim 368 BCE, and there are various suggestions in between. This makes him the near contemporary of a number of other great religious and philosophical pioneers – Confucius (550–470) and Lao Tsu (born *c*.604) in China, Socrates

(469–399) and Plato (427–347) in Greece, Vardhamana Mahavira (c.540–c.468) the founder of Jainism, in India, and various of the later Judaic prophets.

It is tempting to speculate that the Buddha's teaching might have reached and influenced the founding fathers of Western philosophy. He would certainly have approved the Socratic injunction to 'know thyself'. But there is no proof. The most we can point to without solid written or archaeological evidence is a suggestive similarity in the conditions which fostered some of the world's great thought systems – the shift from traditional, agrarian, status-bound societies to more fluid, urban, market economies, with all the attendant opportunities, confusions, anxieties and moral complexities that are thrown up by such a transition. The philosopher Karl Jaspers has called this the 'Axial Age', for it was a pivotal epoch in the history of human awareness and spawned so many philosophies whose concern was change and the moral implications of change.

The story of Siddhartha's birth – in some ornamental gardens in a village called Lumbini – is illuminating for what it does and does not say. The sources make much of the fact that, like the Virgin Mary several centuries later, his mother, Maya, was foretold of her extraordinary destiny in a dream. What has attracted remarkably little comment is the fact that Siddhartha never knew her. For, a week after giving birth, Maya died. It was her sister, Mahaprajapati, who nursed and brought up the baby. I find it very curious that subsequent Buddhist commentators and scholars have made so little of this. No matter how common maternal mortality was in the ancient world, Maya's death must have had a profound effect on her newborn son and his family. It surely suggests a vital clue to Siddhartha's determination to see beyond the limitations of material existence, and the intensity with which he later set out to explore questions concerning life, death and the causes of suffering . . .

Of Siddhartha's early life, his growing up and adolescence, we know very little. Legend has it that he was exceptionally gifted and handsome, but no authentic portraits survive. All the representations of him in statuary and painting date from several centuries later and are highly stylized.

Given his family's rank, the young Siddhartha would have been raised in relative luxury, and with the strong expectation that he would follow in his father's footsteps as a dutiful son and heir. But he must have been something of a rebel, or at least possessed of a restless and seeking spirit, because he refused to take the conventional route – with dramatic consequences.

The legend of his 'renunciation' and 'going forth' is told like this:

King Shuddhodana was so protective and fearful of losing his precious son that he forbade him from stepping beyond the grounds of the palace in which they lived. But Siddhartha decided to defy his father's instructions and secretly ventured out beyond the walls. There he was confronted by four sights which made a profound impression on him. First, he saw a very old man, wizened and decrepit. Second, he observed a person racked with sickness. Third, he witnessed a corpse being taken away for cremation. In short, when Siddhartha left the cosseted environment of the family home, what he encountered was the shocking and painful reality of old age, sickness and death.

The point of the parable is clear. As Siddhartha grew, so did his awareness of the vulnerability of human existence and his sense that there was more to life than the pleasures to be found in his gilded cage. He clearly yearned for a deeper understanding of life in all its manifestations, painful and disturbing as well as comfortable and familiar. If life behind the palace walls symbolizes a state of psychological 'denial', as one biographer has suggested, the 'sights' crystallized a process of exposure and intense questioning.

Siddhartha's fourth journey beyond the palace walls was to be his final one. For on this occasion he had an encounter that would change the course of his life – and human history – for ever. Siddhartha met a shramana.

Shramanas were religious wanderers, renunciants. They lived outside conventional society, moving from place to place as their spirit took them. They had no worldly goods. All they possessed were the clothes in which they stood (some even went naked) and such food as they were given by the people they met on their travels. In this way they sought to free themselves from mundane attachments in order to focus more intently on the spiritual path.

THE POEM OF THE SHRAMANA

Since all the world must be destroyed,
I seek an incorruptible refuge.
I look with equal mind on kinsman and stranger
For longing and hatred have passed from me.
I dwell wherever I happen to be,
At the root of a tree, in temple or on hill,
I seek the good without ties or expectations,
Accepting all that is freely given.[8]

We will never know what it was about the shramana that so captivated Siddhartha – a quality of serenity and composure, perhaps, a sense of something understood? Whatever it was, it must have been deeply impressive, for the young prince decided that he, too, must break from his familiar surroundings and follow the shramana's example if he was to resolve the questions which burned inside him.

Some scriptures say that he was nineteen when he left home, cut off his long hair and gave up his fine robes for the rags and bowl of the mendicant; others that he was nearer twenty-nine, married with a wife, Yashodhara, and a young son, Rahula. Whatever the precise details, it was a profound and dramatic break from everything he knew and had grown up with. His decision to go, in the face of intense pressure, marked a decisive juncture on his journey to enlightenment.

Siddhartha first struck out south, across the great plains of the River Ganges, towards Rajagriha, the main centre of population in the neighbouring state of Magadha. There, in the forests beyond the margins of society, he sought out the two most celebrated meditation teachers of the day, Alara Kalama and Udraka Ramaputra. They taught intensive techniques for enabling the mind to enter a profound state of trance, far beyond the realms of normal consciousness. Siddhartha was, by all accounts, an outstanding student. He worked assiduously and attained the highest level of expertise with exceptional rapidity. But he remained restless, dissatisfied.

Unable to realize the goal of his quest via these particular methods of mental training, he withdrew deeper into the forests and embarked on a rigorous programme of physical self-mortification designed to induce altered states of consciousness. For hours he stood impassively beneath the sun's fierce rays and the lashing monsoon rains, striving by sheer force of will to transcend the sensations of his body. He learned to still his breath for long periods and to quieten his heartbeat until it had all but stopped. He took very little food and water. The effects of these extreme privations was clear for all to see.

My spine stood out like a corded rope, my ribs projected like the jutting rafters of an old roofless cowshed, and the light of my eyes sunk down in their sockets looked like the gleam of water sunk in a deep well.[9]

But still Siddhartha remained unrequited. No study, no teachers, no meditational techniques nor intense austerities seemed capable of yielding the resolution for which he yearned. He sought a more profound awareness. Almost on death's door, for he had starved himself so mercilessly, Siddhartha decided he must reject these extreme methods and leave the forest.

It was a double renunciation. Having once forsaken his family and given up the life to which he had been raised, he now had to abandon his companions and the ascetic path to which he had committed some six years. He must have felt desperately alone. But he had to be true to his quest.

Siddhartha left the forest and washed in a nearby stream. A local village girl, Sujata, offered him some soothing and easily digestible rice boiled in milk, sweetened with wild honey. Slowly he was nursed back to health. In itself this may seem unremarkable, but in terms of what had gone before, the years of reclusive asceticism and self-mortification, it was highly significant. It marked the moment of Siddhartha's return to society. One of his core teachings ever afterwards was about the importance of a balanced approach, avoiding the extremes of excessive indulgence or deprivation: the so-called 'Middle Way'.

The Enlightenment happened shortly thereafter. On the outskirts of a village called Bodh-Gaya, south-west of Rajagriha, seated in deep meditation under the shade of a giant pipal fig tree, Siddhartha attained the goal of his quest. He became the Buddha, the 'awakened one'. The precise date, even the time of year, is impossible to verify. Still less can be known about what he went through, how he felt, what exactly happened on that momentous evening. But it stands for ever as the dramatic climax of the narrative and the pivotal point of his spiritual journey. Everything that has happened subsequently happened because of it. Without it there would be no Buddhism and no Buddhists.

And yet . . . This is the point at which all would-be biographers are forced to admit defeat. For how can one possibly begin to convey an experience which is so far beyond the realm of everyday human consciousness? Any attempt to encapsulate it is bound to be hopelessly inadequate.

We can state with confidence that the Buddha experienced a series of profound, life-transforming realizations on the basis of intensive meditation, and that this process involved an acute psychological battle against the forces of negativity and distraction (the legend goes into lurid detail about the many ways in which he was tempted to abandon his course by his 'devilish' adversary, Mara); but this is to render the richness and profundity of the experience one-dimensional and trite.

The schematic 'description' offered in the traditional accounts scarcely gets us much further:

> He entered into the knowledge of previous existences in the first watch of the night; in the second watch he purified his divine eye; and in the final watch gained an insight into the knowledge of the interdependent causal origins.[10]

In other words, Siddhartha first looked back into the furthest past. He concentrated his mind on all the changes in the universe from the remotest depths of time, took stock of his 'entire life' up to that point, seeing it as part of a continuous, unbroken chain of events, of innumerable successive births and rebirths. He 'recollected' himself.

In the 'second watch' Siddhartha looked forwards into the furthest future – in other words, the same process in reverse – reinforcing this sense of an unbroken chain of events in time, endless links of causes and effects and effects and causes stretching on and on. He 'saw' how all his intentions and actions had moral effects and moral consequences, good and bad, creative and destructive.

In the third and critical phase of the meditation, Siddhartha fused and deepened the two preceding insights. With his whole being he realized the essential relationship between past, present and future, the connectedness of all aspects of existence throughout time. He understood the 'fundamental interdependence of things', and with it the key to happiness.[11]

> He . . . entered the great ocean of life in which all distinctions of mind and body, self and environment are entirely eliminated . . . He experienced a dynamic, moment-to-moment sense of his own being and all phenomena around him undergoing formation and disintegration in perfect harmony with the rhythm of formation and disintegration manifested by the cosmic life. In other words, he grasped the eternal truth that the rhythm of the cosmic life supported, at the core, his own being and all phenomena . . . Shakyamuni awakened to this mystic reality of life in which all things of the universe including human life interrelate, permeate and influence one another.[12]

The truth is that not even a writer of Shakespearean genius could pierce the limits of language and recreate what happened under the pipal tree. Of all the noble attempts at this impossible task I recommend chapter four of Jinananda's *Warrior for*

Peace. It is a stunning piece of imaginative reconstruction — and that is as much as it ever can be. For if we could truly experience what the Buddha went through on that night we would be Buddhas ourselves.

It may, however, be possible to approach an understanding by analogy. There are examples of illuminating breakthroughs in the Western, scientific tradition: Archimedes leaping out of his bath and shouting 'Eureka', for instance, or James Watt staring at a kettle of boiling water and suddenly grasping the potential of steam power. Isaac Newton, like Siddhartha, is supposed to have had his dramatic and profound realization about gravity while sitting beneath a tree.

These were all turning points in the history of world thought and they have interesting features in common with the story of Siddhartha's enlightenment. First, they all came as revelations, 'out of the blue'. At least, that is how they are described, and there is no reason to doubt the immediacy of the experience. Second, although the breakthrough itself occurred instantaneously and with dramatic force, it was preceded by years of intense study, immersion, observation and gruelling experiment. It may be attributed to 'genius', but it derived from assiduous application. Third, these seekers after truth did not find anything that had not been there before. Theirs was a discovery not an invention. Their genius consisted in realizing for the first time something that had been in front of them all along. It was as if they perceived a deeper layer of reality, a glimpse of the underlying structure of the phenomenal world.

The difference between Archimedes, Watt, Newton and Siddhartha is that, whereas the scientists achieved a profound insight into their physical environment, Siddhartha experienced enlightenment in terms of a universal truth about the human condition — the very nature of life itself. He 'saw' how life comes about and how it ceases, how all things arise, grow, decay, die and arise again in an endless sequence. He realized that nothing in the universe is permanent: everything is in a state of flux. And it was from this point onwards that he understood the fundamental human problem: the suffering we experience because of our inability to come to terms with the true, transitory nature of existence. Siddhartha had become a Buddha.

What the Buddha Did Next

If the story had simply ended there we would be none the wiser. There would have been no one to recount the tale and record it for subsequent generations, no one to bear witness, no audience, no followers, no students, no supporters, no powerful patrons, no one to pass on the flame – in short, no Buddhists.

What the Buddha did next, therefore, was decisive. He embarked on a second, even longer journey. After so many ordeals, and having finally resolved his life's quest, he might have been forgiven for deciding to rest where he was, or return home and settle back down with his family. Indeed, the sources say he weighed these possibilities seriously in the weeks after his enlightenment. But he eventually rejected these options. For the remainder of his life (some forty-five years) he became a teacher. As before he travelled constantly. This time, however, he was moved by the desire to help others benefit from the insights he had attained. Like the scientists mentioned above, he *applied* his realisation. It was not Siddhartha, the spiritual explorer, who was the great religious leader: it was Siddhartha, the teacher. His ceaseless concern to pass on to others the benefits of his experience was a hallmark of his compassionate wisdom – the most precious of qualities, which all Buddhists strive to cultivate to this day.

2,500 Years Later . . .

So: how do we get from there to here, from the forests of north India to my desk in north London 2,500 years later? How to span such a vast time and space without recapitulating the whole of Asian history?

I am going to attempt to convey the journey of transmission in three stages: what happened immediately after the Buddha died; how Buddhism made its first great leap beyond the boundaries of India; and, finally, a breakneck gallop down to the present day.

First, the immediate aftermath. Shortly after the Buddha died, his most senior monk, Mahakashyapa, summoned five hundred of the foremost followers to a council, near Rajagriha. There he presided over the compilation of a record of his master's teachings. In this he relied particularly on two monks, Upali and Ananda. Upali recounted the Buddha's guidance on proper monastic conduct. Ananda recalled the Buddha's other teachings.

Ananda was Siddhartha's cousin, and for the last twenty-five years of his life his devoted personal assistant. Thankfully, he was also the possessor of a prodigious memory and was able to recite by heart all of the sutras (sermons or discourses) he had heard over the course of his lifetime's devotion. Presumably the five hundred council members were called upon to authenticate or dispute Ananda's recollection of the most important (or at least the most memorable) of the Buddha's teachings and perhaps supplement or modify them. In this way something approaching an authoritative body of work was established and authorized (though not written down until some centuries later) to be passed on, studied and argued about for posterity.

The words of the Buddha might still have filtered down to us by a million different routes, regardless of the work of the

Council of Rajagriha; but it is difficult to imagine that without a cohesive and formalized body of reference material the Buddhist movement, which was already highly variegated and diffuse, would not have become so attenuated as to lose momentum – and with it the message.

BUDDHIST SCRIPTURES

The Tripitaka or 'Three Baskets' is the name for the collection of scriptures which make up the Buddhist canon. It consists of a threefold collection of sacred texts, comprising, in the European edition, a total of fifty-five volumes (the Bible seems positively brief by comparison). These are:

the Sutra Pitaka or 'Basket of Discourses' containing the teachings and sermons of the Buddha – nineteen texts in thirty-six volumes;

the Vinaya Pitaka or 'Basket of Monastic Discipline' containing the history and rules of conduct for the monastic community, the sangha – four texts in six volumes;

the Abhidharma Pitaka or 'Basket of Higher Teachings' containing scholastic treatises and commentaries analysing the Buddha's teachings – seven texts in thirteen volumes.

The Dhammapada is probably the best known and most widely translated of Buddhist texts. It is an anthology of the Buddha's aphorisms; for example:

As a beautiful flower that is full of hue but lacks fragrance, even so fruitless is the well-spoken word of one who does not practise it. (51)

One may conquer in battle a thousand times a thousand men; yet he is the best of conquerors who conquers himself. (103)

He who holds back rising anger checks a whirling chariot, him I call a real charioteer; other people are only holding the reins. (222)[13]

The second decisive episode occurred some two hundred years later. What a religion needs if it is to succeed – what any body of ideas needs – is an ambitious sponsor and a powerful means of communication: in the jargon of today a 'delivery mechanism'. In our age of globalization, mass media and ever more sophisticated technology, the transformative power of TV, newspapers and the internet is undisputed. The most powerful of these networks are owned by Rupert Murdoch and Bill Gates. They are bolstered by an economic and political system underwritten and policed by the world's only superpower.

Two thousand years ago the dominant power in India was the Mauryan Empire, and its ruler was Ashoka. His conversion to Buddhism was, in my view, critical to its long-term success. The combination of overweening political, economic and cultural power plus a fresh, strong ideology is an irresistible one – as Europe was to discover some five hundred years later when the Emperor Constantine converted to Christianity.

Ashoka ruled from approximately 273–232 BCE. Early in his reign his armies swept all before them, until he ruled almost the entire Indian subcontinent. Then, as the sources record, sickened by the carnage he witnessed after one particularly gruesome campaign, he made a dramatic conversion to

Buddhism, and dedicated the rest of his life to stabilizing his empire on Buddhist principles.

Ashoka had edicts inscribed on tablets and pillars, on rocks and in caves throughout the land. Thirty-three of these have been found to date, providing invaluable information on early Buddhist history. The pillars were often crowned with a distinctive lion capital and set on a round base incorporating a large spoked wheel – symbols of the 'lion's roar' with which the Buddha set in motion the 'wheel of the Dharma' teaching. (The capital of one such pillar, taken from the site of the Buddha's first sermon, became the official emblem of the Republic of India in 1950).

Ashoka's edicts proclaimed Buddhist principles: upright conduct, peacefulness, piety, religious tolerance, respect for parents and teachers, courtesy, charity, self-control and equanimity. A good life, the pillars declared, consisted of 'few bad deeds and many good deeds of kindness, liberality, truthfulness and purity'.[14]

Cynics would doubtless point out that it was politically convenient for Ashoka to have his revelation about the importance of peace having first established his dominion by war. Be that as it may, Ashoka held to his commitment for the rest of his life. Moreover, he matched his deeds to his words. He led pilgrimages to sacred sites, supported all religious traditions throughout his land irrespective of their affiliation, built countless religious monuments or *stupas*, and sponsored missionaries to spread the Buddhist teachings abroad. He sent ambassadors to the Hellenistic world, and his son Mahinda and daughter Sanghamitta travelled to Sri Lanka to establish Buddhism there. He restricted the slaughter of animals, ordered numerous wells to be dug and instigated an extensive tree-planting campaign, lining all the major routes of his empire so that weary travellers could rest in their shade and be comfortable – whether they were reciting Buddhist teachings or not. Ashoka's legacy was profound and far-reaching. (If Bill Gates or Rupert Murdoch happen to pick up this book – please take note.)

Ashoka died in c.232 BCE. That still leaves some 2,238 years to cover, over two millennia in which Buddhism continued to expand numerically and geographically. Whether or not this success was in some sense 'inevitable' is a debate which can be had elsewhere (by the thirteenth century it had all but died out in its homeland, India, as a result of a renaissance in Hindu thought and a series of destructive Muslim invasions). My concern here is to bring the story up to date, so let me simply tell you about my connection with it.

I learned about Buddhism from my next-door neighbour over the course of innumerable cups of coffee and jazz music sessions. He is a member of a Buddhist organization called Soka Gakkai International, based in Japan but with groups all round the world. Apparently (for I never met her) the first Buddhist from this particular group to come to Britain was a woman called Etsuko, who married a milkman called Bob Lynch and moved to Oxford in 1959. Mrs Lynch learned her Buddhism at a time when Josei Toda, a publisher and businessman, headed the organization in Tokyo. His mentor was Tsunesaburo Makiguchi, a pioneer educator who found in Buddhism a resonance with his theories of what would now be called child-centred learning and who had started a group called Soka Kyoiku Gakkai (Value Creating Education Society) in 1937. Soka Gakkai was based on the teachings of the thirteenth-century Japanese sage, Nichiren. Nichiren had studied at Mount Hiei, the head temple of the Tendai sect whose founder was Chih-I. Chih-I's works on Buddhism had originally come to Japan from China in the latter half of the eighth and beginning of the ninth century via the scholar monk Saisho (aka Dengyo) a student of Chih-I's protégé, Miao-Lo. Chih-I based his seminal classification of the Buddha's teachings on the translations of Kumarajiva (350–409). Kumarajiva's was widely regarded as the best translation of the Sanskrit edition of the scriptures. He was influenced by the great Indian scholar, Nagarjuna who lived in the second century. The sutras, or teachings of the Buddha, were first recorded by Siddhartha's cousin and devoted personal assistant, Ananda, as we have seen. So these individuals, Ananda, Nagarjuna, Kumarajiva, Chih-I, Miao-Lo, Saisho, Nichiren, Makiguchi, Toda, Mrs Lynch and Rory McInroy I regard as my spiritual ancestors, my eleven degrees of separation from that moonlit night under the pipal tree.

Every other Buddhist alive today will have his or her own unique lineage should they choose to investigate it. From this highly selective genealogy I have omitted about twenty generations of high priests whose names I could find out but haven't, plus countless thousands of people whose names I will never know but whose words formed part of the conversation. The way I've described my own family tree may well be inaccurate but, in the absence of a laboratory-authenticated spiritual DNA test, we will never know for sure. The fact is that somehow the message got through from the Buddha to me – and now I am about to transmit it to you.

4

What did the Buddha teach?

All Change

Nothing lasts for ever. Strive hard to work out your
enlightenment.

These were the Buddha's last words. There have been many
different translations of this statement[15] but they all contain the
same essential three messages: (1) that everything in life is subject to change; (2) that there is, implicitly at least, a means of
understanding this process and becoming freer and happier;
(3) that it is a project which requires urgent attention.

The last point is not difficult to grasp. The Buddha led by
example. His quest involved prodigious courage and commitment. By passing on the benefits of his experience through his
teachings he may have spared his followers some of the hard
work – but not all. For that was his journey: this is ours. He
blazed the trail, but we still have to walk it for ourselves, to
make it our own. We each have a unique set of issues to deal
with. Some of them are relatively easy to resolve; many are
more difficult. But if we are to use our precious existence to the

full we must attend to them diligently and as a matter of urgency.

The first proposition – that nothing lasts for ever, or, as it is more classically expressed, 'decay is inherent in all composite things' – takes us to the heart of Buddhist metaphysics. It is an analysis which is simple, profound and extraordinarily modern. Like quantum physics and relativity theory, Buddhism holds that everything is changing all the time. Some changes are immediate and obvious, like the evanescent expressions on a baby's face. Others – the height of a mountain range or the outline of the coast, for example – only become apparent after a very long time. But nothing stands still or lasts for ever. There is no such thing as permanence. The Sanskrit term for this concept is *anitya*.

There is no such thing as permanence because there is no such thing as absolute substance. Objects may appear on the surface to have fixed physical properties: shape, weight, solidity. In reality, at a deeper level of magnification, they are made up of lots of smaller components, minute bundles of dynamic energy: granules, atoms, molecules, subatomic particles, and so on. This is what is meant by all things being 'conditioned' or 'composite'. Nothing is fixed. Nothing is what it seems.

And nothing is separate. Everything is connected. People love to think of themselves as individuals. The human ego seems to have a vested interest in bolstering the view of a separate existence, a world 'out there'. But nothing happens in isolation. Phenomena that may appear distinct are, in fact, fundamentally connected. Change in one area causes change in others. When the butterfly of chaos theory flutters its wings on the other side of the globe it affects our lives thousands of miles away. Everything is contingent, relative, interdependent.[16]

In short, the world is not stable, or composed of solid, enduring and independent objects: it is in a state of constant flux. Life is continuously arising, disappearing, interacting, melding, decomposing and re-forming. There are not two separate entities, the observer and the observed, the subject and the object. There is only *relationship* – the relationship between all things. This is surely the Buddha's greatest insight, and it was when he grasped its full implications that he finally attained enlightenment.

This understanding of how the natural world is structured has profound implications for the way we appreciate what it is to be human. For, if the Buddha's analysis is correct, we are, in effect, hallucinating most of the time, seduced by the world of appearances and out of touch with deeper reality. If change is the only constant, there can be no such thing as a permanent 'Self', Soul, 'core reality', call it what you will.[17] To this key teaching Buddhist scholars have given the name *anatman*, meaning 'no fixed self'.

Human existence, according to Buddhism, is not an entity: it is a process. The physical body reconstitutes itself in its entirety over the course of a seven-year period. The mind changes even more rapidly. There is nothing external under-pinning the process of existence. Nor is it internally fixed or autonomous in any way. As the saying goes, 'You cannot step in the same river twice.' We can see immediately that the river never stands still. The Buddha's great insight was that the 'You' who is standing in the river is changing all the time too.

Such a teaching also introduces a very different way of thinking about how people act and react as they do, and what it is to be a responsible moral agent. In essence, the Buddha analysed human behaviour in the way a modern psychologist might, identifying the drives, motives and impulses which shape our perceptions and lead us to respond in particular ways. As one commentator memorably puts it, 'Buddhism sees human beings as verbs rather than nouns.'[18]

What about the final component in the Buddha's injunction – how to 'work out your enlightenment'? What does it mean to see things as they really are, to be truly fulfilled, happy, free, awakened? This was, after all, his prime concern.

The answer lies in the third of the three *trilakshana* or 'marks of existence': *duhkha*. Duhkha is usually translated as 'suffering' or 'unsatisfactoriness', but I have yet to read a book about Buddhism which doesn't add a disclaimer about the impossibility of rendering it accurately into English. The reason for this is because it has the connotation not only of difficulty but also of change. If impermanence (anitya) is one of the defining characteristics of the physical world, and the psychological realm is no more fixed (anatman), duhkha is the stress this transcience brings in our day-to-day experience.

In other words, we suffer because we do not fully grasp the implication of what it means to be human in a world of flux. We cling to certain good feelings and try to make them last for ever. We recoil from others and try to run away from them. Both instincts, 'attachment' and 'aversion', are understandable; but they miss the point. We will never find true peace until we really understand how to be at home in a world where nothing lasts for ever.

This is not such a difficult concept to comprehend intellectually, especially for people living in modern cities where the pace of change is so rapid that it is clear for all to see. But it does seem to be a difficult proposition for us to accommodate emotionally and to base our lives on. One part of our brain knows that, logically, the universe must be boundless, timeless, infinitely fluid. The other seems to find it reassuring to cling to the psychological equivalent of a fixed, flat-earth view of life – even if it knows that can't really be true.

Perhaps the reasons for this are historical, to do with the

way time has come to be understood in our culture. In the West (and Middle East where the great monotheistic religions Judaism, Christianity and Islam were born) time is viewed as linear – a sequence of distinct events having a beginning, middle and end. In the East, however, time is thought of as patterned, cyclical even. Where Western history has tended to be studied as a drama which has a direction – and a Director – in the East past, present and future are inextricably intertwined. Western cosmologies teach that the universe came into being as the result of a unique act of creation, the scientific version of which is the Big Bang. By contrast, the Indian culture which spawned Buddhism located itself in a cosmos that had always existed, undergoing vast cycles of growth and decline, expansion and contraction, lasting billions of years.

Buddhists don't, therefore, require God or Allah to explain the origins of the universe. There is no need to invoke an all-powerful Creator to get the world rolling, no need for a cosmic virgin birth. In this respect Buddhism seems very modern. But the big questions of where we come from and what happens to us when we die[19] can only be deferred not despatched. They remain very awkward for Buddhists too. The time has come to approach the most controversial aspect of Buddhist teaching – the idea of rebirth and karma.[20]

Rebirth and Karma

Ancient Indian cosmology echoed the rhythms of nature. Just as day follows night, the moon waxes and wanes, the tides rise and fall, the seasons come and go, and just as the agricultural cycles of germination, growth, shedding and renewal are repeated year after year, so it seemed natural for many Indian thinkers to picture human life as following a similar pattern, passing through an extended series of births and deaths. To this process they gave the name *samsara*, which literally means 'flowing on'. Individual existences were thought of 'like pearls on an infinitely long necklace, each one separate but strung together in an endless series'.[21] This was the world into which the Buddha was born, a world in which belief in rebirth was widespread.

The traditional Buddhist schema, shaped by this ancient cosmology, sets out six possible realms of rebirth: hell, the animal kingdom, the realm of 'hungry ghosts' (*preta*), the realm of 'demons' (*asura*), the human world, and the heavens – home to the gods (*deva*). These realms are not, strictly speaking, arranged in a simple hierarchy because movement between them is more flexible than a linear model would imply, but it is clear that inhabiting the realm of the gods is distinctly preferable to living in hell (or rather hells – some sources speak of there being ten hot and ten cold varieties), a realm of intense anguish and torment.

Readers who live with a pampered cat may disagree, but rebirth in the animal kingdom is generally considered undesirable since animals have little control over their destiny and often fall prey to others – the most rapacious of all being *homo sapiens*.

Another possible realm for rebirth is that of the 'hungry ghosts'. These are unhappy, shadowy spirits bound to the earth by their strong desires, condemned to hover around the fringes of the human world watching others indulge in the pleasures they once enjoyed.

A fourth realm is home to the demigods or 'demons', a race of supernatural beings who have their origins in ancient Indian mythology and resemble the warlike Norse gods, Thor and Odin. Driven by anger, enmity, lust for power and vengeance, they are locked in perpetual conflict, condemned to fight battles which never reach a conclusive end.

Fifth comes the human world. Rebirth as a human being is regarded as both desirable and difficult to attain: desirable because humans can consciously work to change their future and are ideally placed to see into the nature of existence at a number of levels – mental, physical, spiritual; difficult because it is so rare to be born as a human being.

Sixth is the realm of the gods, beings who live in bliss – though they, too, are born and reborn like everyone else. The upper levels of the heavens (there are gradations even within this dimension) are increasingly sublime and the lifespans of the gods increase at each stage, extending in many cases to millions of years. But the gods, too, must beware, for they can be lulled into complacency and self-absorption by the ease of their existence and forget that it is temporary and has to be earned.

But isn't Buddhism supposed to be non-theistic? Yes, in the sense that the 'gods' it describes are no more fixed or immutable than human beings are. They are not absolute, or eternal, or above or beyond natural law. But no, if non-theism is taken as implying materialism. Buddhism sees life as operating on a number of levels, with varying degrees of physical embodiment, so it is quite comfortable with the idea of a pantheon of subtle energies – perhaps akin to the Christian and Muslim notion of angels.

For my part, given that I have no personal interest in ghosts or out-of-body experiences or supernatural phenomena, I prefer to interpret the gods, and indeed the realms of rebirth, in naturalistic, psychological terms. In this respect I am drawn to the interpretation offered by Nichiren Buddhism, which depicts ten worlds or realms rather than six and understands them as representing different 'states of life'. Thus, for example, hell connotes extreme personal suffering and the animal world represents brute instinct.

Moreover, Nichiren Buddhism sees all these worlds as having both positive and negative qualities. For instance, the experience of hellish suffering can be used to encourage and support other people who are in dire straits; anger can be harnessed in defence of a just cause; acting on instinct, one can be responsive and courageous as well as impetuous and rivalrous. The ten worlds are also intermeshed, changing all the time and affecting each other, so that in the course of a day, or even an hour, one may experience glimpses of all ten.[22]

The Ten Worlds	State of Life
hell	extreme suffering
hunger	insatiable desire
animality	brute instinct
anger	conflict
humanity	calm
rapture	overwhelming joy
learning	self-reflection
absorption	realization
bodhisattva	caring for others
buddhahood	enlightenment

The Ten Worlds of Nichiren Buddhism

This is just one of a number of interpretations. Not all Buddhists take the traditional teachings at face value. Some have begun to question the belief in rebirth entirely and are exploring new interpretations which are not tied to the worldview of the classical sources. For others, belief in rebirth is fundamental, for without it the entire edifice of Buddhist metaphysics is undermined.[23]

An excellent book which goes into the debate with great clarity is *Exploring Karma and Rebirth*, by Nagapriya.[24] The linkage of these two concepts is fundamental to most accounts of Buddhism – and inescapably awkward for those who find the idea of rebirth problematic.

The term 'karma' is often misused in modern colloquial expression to imply a kind of fatalism. Its literal translation is very different. It means, quite simply, 'action'. All actions have consequences: all consequences have further repercussions, and so on . . . What the Buddha realized when he became enlightened was that nothing exists eternally in and of itself. All phenomena are the result of prior activity. Something has caused them to be. And all phenomena in turn cause other things to happen. They create effects.[25] This is the doctrine which is variously translated as 'dependent origination' (*pratitya-samutpada*), 'dependence in origination', 'conditioned arising' or 'conditional genesis'. I think of it simply as the fundamental interdependence of things.[26]

We live, so the teaching goes, in a world of causes and effects. On a day-to-day level few people would dispute this. If we exercise we get fitter. If we drink too much alcohol we get a headache. If we lie out in the sun without protection we get burnt. But even this is not simple. Some people get more burnt than others. Some smoke heavily and seem to be fine, while others get lung disease for no apparent reason. The situation becomes so much more complicated when the debate enters the moral realm. It is far too easy to rush to a crass and simplistic judgment, as the former England football manager, Glenn Hoddle, proved when he spoke of disabled children having done something wrong in a previous lifetime. Is it necessarily a punishment to be born disabled? Which Christopher Reeve was the superman – the millionaire actor in tights or the indefatigable paraplegic? It is as difficult to fathom a person's karma as it would be to describe the stucture of their DNA simply by looking at them in the street.

What Buddhists seek to do in their lives is make 'good' causes – that is, causes which are conducive to enlightenment – and refrain from 'bad' causes or habits (karmic patterns could be seen as habitual ways of thinking and behaving) which lead to suffering. They thereby accrue what is termed *punya*, usually translated as 'merit'.

But, once again, it is not always easy to evaluate the rights and wrongs of a situation or to see how the law of cause and effect is operating. What explains attrocities for example? If the universe is a just and orderly rather than random and chaotic place, why do seemingly innocent people suffer? After the mass-killing of the school children in Beslan, the Archbishop of Canterbury was challenged on BBC radio to explain how God could have 'allowed' such a thing to happen. Buddhists might not have to formulate the question in this way but they do have to make sense of the moral outrage somehow. What had the children 'done' to explain such suffering? In what sense was it a result of their karma?

Buddhists would point, I think, to the circumstances which created the desire on the part of the terrorists to perpetrate such an act. And they would focus on the need to counter such violence and anger in human beings with wisdom and compassion. There is no difference in this respect from other religions of course; but the Buddhist emphasis would be on looking inside ourselves first, for a human rather than super-human explanation.

As to the karma of the children themselves, could it simply be that they were in the wrong place at the wrong time, dragged into a situation which was not (consciously at least) of their making? The difficulty – and it is a critically important diffi-culty – is that some karma is so deep-seated that it is impossible to interpret its effects. We can never know the full context. A myriad concatenating causes will throw up all sorts of conse-quences for which there is no clear explanation.

We will almost certainly never know in this lifetime (not in a way we can 'prove' at least) how karma operates or whether rebirth is truth or an illusion. Some people swear they can recollect previous lives; others say this is pure fantasy. According to a recent poll nearly a quarter of Britons and Americans believe in some form of reincarnation. Three-quarters evidently don't.

Nor will we ever know how systematized a view of rebirth the Buddha had. His teachings contain little precise informa-tion on the subject. He discouraged speculation about it. Indeed, it was in response to such a question that the Buddha told the parable of the poisoned arrow with which this book began. On another occasion he turned the question back on the questioner: 'Where does a flame go when it is blown out?' The flame, he went on, does not 'go' anywhere: it is simply the process of combustion that ceases.

Fire imagery features quite often in Buddhist teachings. Nirvana, the end of samsara, literally means 'quenching' or 'blowing out,' in the way that a thirst is slaked or the flame of a candle is snuffed. What is extinguished is the 'triple fire' of the 'three poisons': greed, hatred and ignorance. There is no more craving, no more anger, no more delusion. The obsession with selfish concerns drops away and is transformed into a state of awareness characterized by deep joy and refinement. Negative emotions, doubts, worries, anxieties and fears evaporate. The mind is finally clear and at peace.

Beyond nirvana in this lifetime, according to the traditional accounts, was the 'entry into nirvana' (*parinirvana*) which the Buddha was supposed to have attained when he died and from whence he would never be reborn in human form. Where did he go to then? We're back to the question about the flame. The texts talk of nirvana beyond death as 'the furthest shore', a state of being which is 'unborn, unoriginated, uncreated and unformed'. Such language is frustratingly enigmatic. But what else could it be, given that it is beyond the realm of human experience? It was, according to the Buddha, one of the 'great inexpressibles'. To follow this line of inquiry was not only futile but positively unhelpful and 'not conducive to enlightenment'. We would find out in due course what happens in the future. The point was to stop suffering in the here and now.

It is important to underline this advice because Buddhism is often, wrongly, portrayed as passive, fatalistic or even pessimistic. The Law of Cause and Effect does not imply any of these outlooks. Quite the opposite. Its operation is neither random nor chaotic. It is patterned and structured. Striving to see its pattern and to act accordingly is the key to becoming enlightened. If karma is action, and action is based on moral choice (*cetana*), Buddhism requires us to take absolute responsibility for what we do in the here and now, because how we act in the present will help determine what happens to us in the future.

Moreover, it is important to scotch the notion that the idea of rebirth was a desperate human invention to stave off the fear of death, a panacea of some sort. The Buddha, like the other Indian thinkers of his age, found the idea of endless rebirth uncomfortable. Far from being welcome, it meant repeatedly suffering the pains of birth and death, sickness and ageing, separation and loss. The challenge, as he and his contemporaries saw it, was not how to live for ever but how to escape from the relentless cycle of existence in samsara. Some sought to do this by intensive meditation that went beyond and ignored the body; others by pushing the body to its limits in the hope of glimpsing a transcendent reality beyond birth and death. The Buddha experimented with these methods himself, as we have seen, but he did not find them ultimately satisfactory. The solution he arrived at was altogether more practical.

5

The Four Noble Truths

Finding the Path

> And what have I declared?
> 'This is suffering' – I have declared.
> 'This is the origin of suffering' – I have declared.
> 'This is the cessation of suffering' – I have declared.
> 'This is the way leading to the cessation of suffering' – I have declared.[27]

Clear, cogent and deceptively simple, the Buddha encapsulated his teaching in 'Four Noble Truths'. He sometimes compared himself to a physician, and his diagnosis and prescription are set out much in the manner of a clinical assessment. The first Noble Truth examines the condition, the second explores its causes, the third concludes that a cure is possible, and the fourth prescribes the remedy.

Unlike many modern doctors, the Buddha wasn't primarily interested in surface symptoms. For the cure to be effective it must work from the inside out. The 'patient' must get at the underlying causes of their suffering and take responsibility for their recovery by adopting a new regime for daily life, a fundamental change in attitude and lifestyle.

In our age of international jet travel, lunchtime liposuction and Las Vegas marriages this may not be a fashionable message – but it is the truth. Quick 'fixes' rarely last. Changing karma is not a cosmetic process. It means understanding our hidden motives and most deeply entrenched patterns, seeing the way our unconscious conditioning affects how we think of ourselves, and getting to grips with the way we conduct our lives.

The **First Noble Truth**, the Truth of Suffering (*duhkha*), states that difficulty and disappointment are inescapable aspects of human experience. Birth can be a painful process; and so, more often, is the decline into death. No one is immune from illness, whatever the wonders of modern medicine. Suffering also includes emotional and psychological distress, which is no less real for being invisible. There isn't a person in the world, rich or poor, famous or unknown, who will not experience grief and sorrow at some point in their life, and conditions such as depression are often chronic and more difficult to treat than physical illnesses.

Beyond these obvious examples, the First Noble Truth refers to a more mundane kind of dis-ease: the day-to-day frustration of dashed hopes and expectations. At best these disappointments are annoying. At worst they may result in profound disenchantment and a corrosive feeling of failure and inadequacy. Even when suffering is not acute or dramatic there can be all sorts of lower-level unhappiness which are distressing and debilitating. One need look no further than the prodigious consumption of Valium and Prozac in the modern world for proof of its ubiquity.

If life is, by its very nature, difficult the **Second Noble Truth**, the Truth of Arising (*samudaya*), explains that suffering comes about from craving or 'thirst' (*trishna*) for things to be other than they are. Either we have something we don't want – a headache or an overdraft, for example – or we don't have something we *do* want – a fast car, say, or the 'perfect' partner. Craving is said to fuel suffering in the way that wood stokes a flame. In one teaching known as the Fire Sermon, the Buddha spoke of all human experience as being 'ablaze' with desire and infatuation. Fire spreads rapidly, always consuming what it feeds on. Craving is the same. It is never satisfied.

The Second Noble Truth states that craving manifests itself in three main forms. The first is thirst for sensual pleasure (*kama*): the constant desire to experience new tastes, sensations, smells, sights and sounds. The second is thirst for existence (*bhava*): the deep instinctual will to hang on to life at all costs. The third is the urge to negate, avoid, reject and even to destroy (*vibhava*) that which seems unpleasant or alien: a form of extreme 'denial' or aversion as a modern psychologist might say.

So does this mean that all desire is wrong? We are, after all, creatures with appetites. Many seem positively beneficial – wanting to feed one's family or to heal the sick for example . . . No: what the Buddha is speaking about here is desire that has become twisted or unbalanced in some way, either because it is excessive or because it is mis-directed. Above all, he is referring to the desires to which we find ourselves attached (which may even include the obsessive drive to do good for others while neglecting ourselves or those nearest us). We can't seem to shake these desires off. They have somehow – often subtly – become addictive. We are hooked.

Desire becomes negative the moment it takes on an addictive

aspect. It starts to cause pain to oneself and to others. And it begins to bind us ever more tightly to the very difficulty we are trying to escape. Like a greedy child who can only remove his hand from a sweet jar by letting go of the sweet, grasping will only make our situation worse. We need to know both when to hold on and when to let go. When Buddhism talks about 'non-attachment' it emphatically does not mean indifference.

The **Third Noble Truth**, the Truth of Cessation (*nirodha*), offers the possibility of hope. For if suffering has a cause, it follows logically that the means must also exist to stop, remove or transform the cause. If the root of suffering is attachment to false ideas, grasping onto things we can't have, or failing to come to terms with the way things really are, then the solution is to resolve that ignorance, let go, get real.

In order to be happy we need to understand that change is inherent in all things, abandon our fantasy of trying to control it or stop it happening, see it more clearly for what it really is – a natural process. We also need to root out the 'three poisons' – greed (*raga*), hatred (*dvesha*) and delusion (*moha*) – and replace them with something more valuable. Understanding how they operate is the key to transforming suffering.

Our experience of these poisons and the suffering they cause will be unique to each of us, wrapped up in our own particular bundle of personal relationships; but wherever there is suffering or the memory of unhappiness, evidence of one of the poisons will be close by. The fundamental task of Buddhism is to understand, undermine and neutralize these poisons. More than that, they need to be transformed into their opposites – generosity and non-attachment, compassion and loving kindness, wisdom and understanding – the 'three qualities' of the Buddha.

What is it to be non-attached? What is it to be compassionate? What is it to be wise? How do we cultivate these qualities?

By living in the right way, developing and constantly refining the necessary skills. These are the techniques set out in the **Fourth Noble Truth**. It describes the route from samsara to nirvana. It consists of eight factors divided into three categories: morality (*shila*), meditation (*samadhi*) and wisdom (*prajña*). This is the so-called Noble Eightfold Path. Lama Surya Das's publisher has renamed it the 'Eight Steps to Enlightenment'. This is, strictly speaking, an inaccurate title. Rather than stepping stones or rungs on a ladder which are stepped on and then left behind, the components of the path continuously inform each other every step of the way. But it is a wonderfully helpful and uplifting book and a great companion on any journey.

THE NOBLE EIGHTFOLD PATH

Prajna

Right View means accepting the Four Noble Truths. Not blind acceptance or complete understanding, but rather receptiveness to the teachings and a willingness to examine them in the light of our own experience.

Right Resolve means making a serious commitment to develop the qualities of wisdom and compassion, together with a corresponding determination not to be distracted from the path.

Shila

Right Speech means telling the truth with sensitivity, speaking in a way which doesn't hurt or divide others, avoiding gossip and idle chatter.

Right Action means abstaining from harmful behaviour such as killing, stealing or abusing sensual pleasures.

Right Livelihood means not engaging in an occupation which causes hurt to others through the use of wrong speech or wrong action.

Samadhi

Right Effort means gaining control of one's thoughts, restraining negative states of mind and replacing them with positive ones.

Right Mindfulness means cultivating constant awareness of one's body, feelings, mental states and thoughts.

Right Meditation means developing deep levels of calm and insight through various techniques which concentrate the mind and integrate the personality.

6

From Dharma to Sangha

Buddhism after the Buddha

> I go to the Buddha for refuge, I go to the Dharma for refuge, I
> go to the Sangha for refuge.[28]

Buddhism abounds with numbers – the eightfold path, the six
perfections, the five precepts, the four noble truths . . . Above
all, it goes in for the number three. To the three marks of existence, the three poisons and the three qualities, let us now add
two further trinities – the 'three turnings of the wheel' and the
'three jewels'. For in describing them we can outline the story
of how the Buddha's followers came to understand themselves
as a community and what happened to his teachings as a
consequence.

When the Buddha preached his first sermon, in a deer park
in Sarnath, near the town of Benares, the scriptures say that he
set in motion the 'wheel of the Dharma'. Dharma means 'the
Buddha's teaching'. And since what the Buddha taught was neither an invention nor an interpretation, but rather what he had
discovered as the result of his enlightenment, dharma means, by

extension, the way things are, the way the world works, the Law of Life.

The first people to hear the Buddha's teaching were five companions from his days as an ascetic. To start with they were reluctant to speak to him (they had been very upset when he had decided to part company with them and leave the forests). But they were intrigued by the transformation they observed in him and soon found themselves captivated as he began to recount his recent experiences and insights. Word spread quickly. People from all walks of life (even the local king, Bimbisara) came to hear the new teacher speak. In no time a group of 'disciples' had emerged. These formed the nucleus of a *sangha*, or community of adherents, the third of what are called the three Buddhist 'jewels' – Buddha, Dharma, Sangha.

Many of them chose to accompany the Buddha on his teaching journeys. When the monsoon rains made travel difficult they would spend time in retreat, often in simple accommodation on land donated by the laity or in parks on the outskirts of towns and villages. As they returned year after year, these centres (known as *viharas*) became semi-permanent and ultimately evolved into autonomous, self-governing monasteries where monks could take up full-time residence. It was an arrangement with advantages for everyone. Since their material needs were met, the monks could devote more time to meditation and study; while for the lay community the monastery provided much-needed medical and educational support and a focal point for religious practice.

The monastic community continued to rely on donations from the laity. As time went on these included legacies of land and property as well as money. Since the material needs of the monks were minimal, the wealth of some monasteries increased to the point where they wielded considerable power and influence, and could commission buildings, sculptures and other works of art as patrons in their own right. In this, as in many other respects – for example, the wearing of robes and the practice of shaving the head – Buddhist monasteries resembled the Christian establishments which emerged centuries later in Europe. Indeed, it is tempting to speculate that the concept of monasticism spread from India to the West, though there is no evidence of direct transmission.

The personal testimonies of many monks and nuns who gained enlightenment in this early period have been preserved in a series of texts known as *The Verses of the Elders*. They speak of both the joys and rigours of the monastic life and of the bliss and sense of freedom which suffuses the mind when the path described by the Buddha is followed.

A MONK'S VERSE

How light my body!
Touched by
abundant rapture and bliss,
– like a cotton tuft borne on the breeze
it seems to be floating
– my body!

(*Theragatha* v. 104)

A NUN'S VERSE

So freed! So thoroughly freed am I! –
from three crooked things set
free:

from mortar, pestle,
and crooked old husband.
Having uprooted the craving
that leads to becoming,
I'm set free from ageing and death.

(*Therigatha* v. 11).

At the First Council, held at Rajagriha in the year of the Buddha's death the sangha was relatively unified and able to agree about its master's most important teachings. A century or so later, however, at the Second and Third Councils of Vaisali and Pataliputra, there was no such consensus. Different interpretations of the rules governing monastic life began to emerge. The community started to divide.

The eventual outcome came to be know as the 'Great Schism', a separation into two main factions, one comprising the so-called *Sthaviras* or 'Elders', the other known as the *Mahasamghikas*, or 'Great Assembly'. (Later chroniclers say that the first of these was itself subdivided into eleven schools and the second into seven, making a total of eighteen early schools.) The Sthaviras were the more conservative group: they sought to preserve and practise the Buddha's teaching in its original – and as they argued, purest – form, without modification. The Mahasamghikas were more open to innovation and adaptation in accordance with the times.

Of the original eighteen schools all but one have since died out. The sole survivor is known as the Theravada, which means 'the doctrine of the elders'. Predominant in Sri Lanka, Thailand and Burma, it claims to be descended directly from the original Sthavira community and hence to be the only school which has preserved the Buddha's teachings faithfully down to the present day (a claim which is not undisputed). It is also the only school in which a more or less complete collection of scripture has survived intact from ancient times – the so-called Pali Canon. The Pali language is derived from Sanskrit and regarded as close to the language the Buddha himself might have spoken.

Some time in the two centuries after the reign of Ashoka, a reformist wave ('movement' is probably too strong a term since it was a loose confederation of diverse groups and schools) known as the Mahayana gradually developed. This came to see itself as the second turning of the wheel of the Dharma. Consciously defining themselves against what they pejoratively labelled the Hinayana or 'lesser vehicle' tradition, Mahayanists emphasized the Buddha's active concern to liberate the mass of the people and stressed his teaching of compassion for *all* sentient beings.

New schools proliferated: the Madhyamika school founded by Nagarjuna, the Yogacara school founded by Asanga and Vasubandhu, the Pure Land, Zen and Nichiren schools, to name but a few. Texts such as the 'Perfection of Insight' discourses and the Lotus Sutra had a profound effect on Buddhism's subsequent transmission and development, to the extent that Mahayana was the form of Buddhism which came to predominate in north and east Asia.

Central to the reformist outlook of the Mahayanists was a new, more expansive interpretation of the figure of the bodhisattva. In early Buddhism that term was used more or less exclusively to identify the historical Buddha, Siddhartha Gautama, and it was assumed that only future teachers of equally exceptional status merited such a designation. The bodhisattva, according to this definition, was a kind of proto-Buddha or Buddha-in-waiting. In the Mahayana tradition, however, the term was extended and enhanced. It came to refer to anyone who, rather than focusing on their own personal attainment of nirvana, had decided to dedicate their lives to helping others become enlightened too.

This definition of the bodhisattva implied a radical interpretation of what it is to be a Buddha – a new way of understanding 'Buddha nature'. Its claim, in essence, was that all human beings, irrespective of background, possess the capacity to be Buddhas. The argument in support of this proposition proceeds simply and logically in the following way: if the Buddha was enlightened he must have had the capacity for enlightenment. That capacity cannot simply have emerged from nowhere: it must always have been there. Since he claimed no special or godlike status the same capacity must be inherent in all human beings. Everyone must therefore have the potential for enlightenment by virtue of their common humanity.

This 'Buddha nature' (*Tathagatagarbha*) is not something that is gained or acquired: it has to be revealed. It is like the sun which shines permanently in a blue sky whatever the weather below. We have to break through the clouds of delusion in order to see it. Or, to take another oft-used metaphor, we need to polish the mirror of our lives in order to perceive our Buddha nature more clearly. It takes effort and practice. To this end the bodhisattva is called on to develop and embody the virtues known as the four 'divine abidings' – loving kindness (*maitri*), appreciative joy (*mudita*), equanimity (*upeksa*) and, above all, compassion (*karuna*) – and to practise the Six Perfections (*paramitas*) – generosity (*dana*), morality (*shila*), patience (*kshanti*), resilience (*virya*), meditation (*samadhi*), and wisdom (*prajna*). In this way the *bodhicitta* or 'thought of enlightenment' which lies within each person is activated, cultivated and revealed.

Bodhi means 'enlightenment'. *Citta* is the mind or heart. So, 'the enlightened heart' it could be called. It has two aspects. One aspect is compassion. The other is wisdom – seeing things as they really are. Compassion is usually described as relative *bodhicitta* and wisdom as ultimate *bodhicitta*. It is understood that when you see things as they are in a direct way, then compassion naturally and spontaneously arises, because when you see all the pain that you had before, you understood the true nature of things and realise it to be unnecessary and useless, compassion arises for all the others caught in the pain. Bodhicitta is when wisdom and compassion come together, inseparable.[29]

As well as human bodhisattvas, Mahayana Buddhism also elaborates a collection of colourful celestial beings, sublime and extraordinary entities who have advanced to the end of the bodhisattva path, accumulating great powers en route. They are thought of as inhabiting a 'heavenly' realm, a bit like the angels of Christianity, while remaining attentive to the needs of suffering beings in the mundane world. The best known of these, pre-eminent for his compassion – and for the fact that his dramatic image adorns so much Buddhist art – is Avalokiteshvara (the Dalai Lama is considered to be his present-worldly incarnation). Many demands are made of him and he is capable of responding to all who call upon him in whatever way is most needed. Hence his unmistakable depiction with multiple heads and sometimes as many as a thousand arms.

A final outpouring of Buddhist writings known as the Tantras occurred around the seventh century. These texts promoted new and distinctive techniques for accelerating spiritual progress. A form of Buddhism which became known as the 'diamond vehicle', or Vajrayana, began to emerge from within the Mahayana tradition. This was the third major expression of Buddhist teachings, sometimes identified as the third turning of the wheel of the Dharma.

Vajrayana practices tend to emphasize the power of ritual and are elaborate – almost magical – in form. Extensive use is made of various kinds of *mandalas* (symmetrical diagrams), *mudras* (hand gestures), *mantras* (powerful words) and *dharanis* (incantations). Great stress is laid upon the role of the guru or religious preceptor from whom the student receives direct instruction and initiation. Visualization of a range of holy beings is also important, and a spiritual physiology is elaborated which depicts the human body as made up of a number of channels of energy which can be controlled through yogic exercises in order to develop exceptional powers.

Today Tantra is best known, doubtless pruriently, for its association with sex and sexual yoga – a partial and distorting way of representing the rich body of its teachings about the sacred, liberating power of physicality.

The *Guhyasamaja Tantra*, composed in the early eighth century, is the first Vajrayana text known to contain explicit sexual imagery, symbolizing the attempt to transcend dualism through the fusion of male and female energies. Its appearance was followed by an explosion of similar texts featuring different techniques of sexual yoga. This period also saw the rise of the *maha-siddhas* or 'great adepts', colourful and eccentric characters like Padmasambhava (better known as Guru Rinpoche), who helped transmit the Tantric teachings from India to Tibet and was reputedly the possessor of extraordinary, mystic powers.

Although Vajrayana Buddhism seems to have originated outside monastic circles among unorthodox yogins, it was soon incorporated into the various great centres of Buddhist learning in India, where it gradually became systematized into the now standard fourfold division of *kriya-tantra* (action), *carya-tantra* (performance), *yoga-tantra* (yoga) and *anuttara-yoga-tantra* (supreme yoga). Many of the greatest Indian scholar-monks from the eighth century onwards were Vajrayana adepts. Through their influence Vajrayana Buddhism became widespread, achieving its greatest success in Tibet, Mongolia and China, with the Shingon school as an offshoot in Japan.

Thus, just as Christianity divides between Catholic, Orthodox and Protestant, so Buddhism has three broad traditions: the Southern Buddhism of Sri Lanka and South East Asia where the Theravada is dominant; the Northern Buddhism of Tibet, Mongolia and Bhutan, where the Vajrayana is pervasive; and the Eastern Buddhism of China, Vietnam, Korea and Japan, where various forms of the Mahayana flourish. These are all highly distinctive in their own way, reflecting the differing soils in which they have taken root, the different histories, geographies, cultures and, perhaps most importantly, the different indigenous belief systems with which they melded. A Zen monastery in Korea, spare, austere, silent, would seem on the surface to have very little in common with its Tibetan equivalent, where prayers are accompanied by the banging of drums, the clashing of cymbals and the trumpeting of horns. Given its remarkable diversity of form and expression it is surely to Buddhism's great credit that its 2,500-year history has produced no equivalent to the Christian wars of religion or the Muslim conflicts between Sunni and Shia. The jewel of the sangha is rare and precious precisely because it is so multifaceted.

7

What do Buddhists do?

Life as Meditation

> We are what we think
> Having become what we thought
> Like the wheel that follows the cart-pulling ox
> Sorrow follows an evil thought.
>
> And joy follows a pure thought,
> Like a shadow faithfully tailing a man.
> We are what we think,
> Having become what we thought.[30]

Theory is all well and good, but in the end it is action that matters. In the words of a Buddhist sage: 'You cannot get rich by counting your neighbour's money.'[31] So what do Buddhists actually *do*?

Action, for most Buddhists, begins with meditation.[32] For if action is to have maximum impact and maximum value it must be properly motivated and properly directed. It must be compassionate, wise, focused, right-minded. Meditation is the activity which summons up these qualities. The experiences of some of the Buddhist practitioners at the end of this chapter convey a sense both of the centrality of meditation in their daily lives and of the variety of different practices available.

Why meditating should be a minority activity, regarded as somehow exotic or even odd, says much about the society in which we live. We seem to spend remarkably little time cultivating our most important and distinctive asset. In a world of frenzied and almost all-consuming activity this tendency seems to be on the increase. Every 'labour-saving' device seems to make us 'time poorer'. How have we contrived to fill every second in this way? Are we perhaps afraid of what might happen if we slowed down for a moment? . . .

The results of not examining our hearts and minds before acting are there for all to see: global poverty at a time of unprecedented wealth; global environmental degradation at a time when we have the capability to go to the moon; global terrorism when over a trillion dollars are spent every year on the arms trade. To put it more positively: What wonderful human creation in the world today is not the product of effort, patience, wisdom and generosity of spirit?

So the first and foremost premise of Buddhism is that it is positively worthwhile spending time cultivating our awareness and deeper sensitivity. Meditation is an intensely practical thing to do. Its effects are played out in every aspect of daily life. The word 'spiritual' has done as much damage as good in making mysterious and somehow 'other-worldly' an activity which is designed to be integral and fundamental. 'To be fully alive is to be fully awake.'[33]

Does meditation work? The answer according to those who

practise is Yes. But how to 'prove' that? Scientists haven't yet devised an X-ray for a broken heart, or a litmus which measures compassion. Psychological and neurological research increasingly suggests that meditation has positive benefits, but these are hard to measure under laboratory conditions.[34] We need to experience it for ourselves. We need to do it.

Let's start by exploring very briefly the mechanics of Buddhist meditation. It can take place in a group, with a leader to conduct the process, or it can be practised alone. No incense, bells or candles are necessary. In principle, it can be done anywhere, at any time of day or year. In practice, there are so many distractions that it is useful to establish some kind of structure or routine, even though it's not absolutely necessary. The important thing when starting is not to get sidetracked by seemingly more 'urgent' calls on one's time. As a sage once advised: 'Don't just do something, sit there!'[35]

The most common image of a meditator is of someone sitting cross-legged with eyes closed, back straight and hands gently resting on the knees, but this is just one of many variations. There are silent meditations, walking meditations, chanting meditations, meditations which focus on objects, meditations which don't focus on anything . . . What they all have in common is a process and an aim:

Observing the mind
Calming the mind
Clearing the mind
Focusing the mind

And then taking action or consciously deciding not to react.

So, begin by sitting still somewhere. Try to be quiet. Before long a thought will cross your mind. There's no need to do anything except be aware of it. If you are having a stressful time you will probably observe further thoughts. Worries, doubts and fears may even begin to circle round and round, like a dog chasing its own tail, getting nowhere. There is nothing 'natural' about such negative thought patterns, according to Buddhist teaching. They have been learned or acquired. They can, therefore, be 'unlearned' and replaced with happier, more peaceful and productive states of mind. But first we have to spend time with them, be prepared to look at them, and realize that they are not so bad after all. We have to observe how our mind works.

To do this we have to calm the mind, to collect it and 'bring it home'. The classical form of 'calming' or 'serenity' meditation (*shamatha*), involves focusing on the breath and carefully monitoring (as distinct from attempting to control) the process of respiration. Each full cycle of breathing in and out is counted until a certain number (usually ten) is reached, and then the count begins again at zero. Deceptively simple to describe, it is difficult to complete even a single cycle of this exercise without the mind wandering. When this happens, simply bring the attention back to the breath and resume the exercise.

Other focal objects can be selected apart from the breath – perhaps a physical object such as a flower, a candle or a statue. As the power of concentration is strengthened through daily practice the mind becomes calmer and clearer, more 'together'. The analogy often given is that of a glass of water filled with sediment. If it is constantly agitated it will look cloudy. If it is allowed to settle it will gradually become clearer.

A second kind of technique, insight meditation (*vipashyana*), builds on this. Vipashyana means, literally, 'seeing (as in understanding) things as they really are'. It involves a process of analysis in which the mind, honed by calm, clear concentration comes to perceive the ever-changing flow of experience and to gain a deeper awareness of the power of teachings like the Four Noble Truths, the lack of Self in anything and Dependent Origination. Only by direct realization based on meditative practice can a profound and meaningful insight into these states be acquired.

Traditional Buddhist meditation strategy thus involves a two-pronged approach: calming meditation trains the emotions, while insight meditation refines the mind. Both these aspects of the personality must be developed in harmony if our full potential is to be unlocked.

Many other kinds of meditation have been developed down the centuries. A good one to practise is visualization, a technique which is very popular in the Tantric-influenced schools. The key is to meditate on an image, typically a picture or statue of a Buddha, until a vivid replica, complete in every detail, is created in the mind, to the extent that you can exchange place with the image and 'become' the Buddha you have created. Similar techniques are used today in a secular context by high achievers like athletes, footballers and even super-salespeople who, as part of their training, visualize themselves winning races, scoring goals or clinching big deals. By experiencing the results vividly in the imagination it becomes easier to bring them into reality. The mind is infinitely flexible. It will respond to whatever information it is given. The 'inner game' is there for all of us to play.

Buddhism makes available a wide range of methods and spiritual techniques which are appropriate for different personality types and different needs. Discussion with an experienced teacher will usually reveal which method is most appropriate for the beginner. Whatever the technique adopted, however, the overall strategy is to re-orientate ourselves psychologically, making progress day by day towards a happier and more fulfilled life. Gradually our outlook becomes restructured and our demeanour and behaviour with it. Head and heart become better integrated. We feel calmer and able to concentrate for longer. We spend more time living in the moment, less being distracted. We're happier.

The results should be clear for all to see. Some surface changes can be very rapid and striking. There are no 'quick fixes' or short cuts, however, when it comes to changing deeper patterns of response which have probably been reinforced by years of negative conditioning. It requires time, patience and commitment, not unlike the process of learning a musical instrument. Perhaps this is the reason more people don't meditate. It takes consistent effort and perseverance, and humans don't seem very good at that, especially after a hard day in the office or when there are so many other glittering distractions. But persistence is the only way to create something of lasting value. Meditation doesn't cost anything and the rewards can be considerable.

Varieties of Buddhist Experience

In order to convey some sense of how different Buddhists use their practice I interviewed a number of people from differing traditions and asked each in turn the following question: 'What difference do you believe your practice makes in your daily life?'

Here is what they said:

'I try to spend time every day *being* rather than *doing*. I've spent too much time in the past rushing around frantically and not enough taking stock, allowing things to get integrated and absorbed properly. So I try to make sure to safeguard some time every day to catch my breath and pause to enjoy the moment – even if this means just sitting quietly on the sofa after work with a cup of tea. I suppose you could say that my formal practice is an attempt to become more aware of the quality of my experience more of the time.'

'I come from a Buddhist family in a predominantly Buddhist country (Sri Lanka) so it is difficult for me to imagine what it might be like not to be a Buddhist! But I do seem to have a different outlook from many of my non-Buddhist friends. Possibly I'm less anxious and less materialistic . . . You'll have to ask them!'

'There are some times when I manage to get beyond my thoughts and look at deeper structures and patterns and how this relates to what I've learnt from Buddhist teachings – but this tends to happen more when I'm on retreat and doing more intensive meditation.'

'My basic practice is trying to establish continual awareness, primarily of my shifting emotional states. Over the last thirty years this has undoubtedly clarified my perceptions, resulted in less self-centred behaviour, and given me greater peace of mind in the adversities and discomfitures of life. It has made me more "easeful" both with myself and others. The foundation for this round-the-clock practice is a meditation of about an hour each day. It is also reinforced by going on several week-long group retreats and solitary retreats each year. Reading inspiring literature is valuable. Also helpful to me are the several workshops which I facilitate each year. In these I have to clarify my own insights and ideas, and I learn much, in heart and head, from the participants. Finally there is the encouraging and supportive fellowship of Sangha – my many Dharma friends.'

'Running a small business requires many attributes – a clear sense of priorities, the ability to be focused, to communicate better, to be "aware" of each other, to work together effectively, to think in a lucid and creative way – and there is no doubt that my practice helps here. In more personal terms, I hope I'm a better listener that I used to be and more present in my own life and choices. I don't earn much money (that's an understatement) but I feel the way I live is much richer, freer and more balanced than the life I used to have.'

'My practice gives me a feeling of access to an infinite power of compassion which undergirds my life. Many years ago I felt that I was "stuck". I did not have any feeling of progress, and was not even sure if progress was possible. That is when I discovered the teaching of the Infinite Buddha Power, which accepts me just as I am, and this has transformed my life.'

'My practice is very simple. I chant to express gratitude and appreciation for my life, remember my teachers and ancestors, transform my negativity into creativity, and pray for peace throughout the world and the happiness of all living beings. No priests are involved. No elaborate rituals are necessary. No money has to be paid. Ceremony is kept to a minimum. We hold meetings in each other's homes and try to get involved in the local community, to "create value". That's what it's all about in a nutshell. Belief is one thing, but taking action to create value is what really counts.'

'My belief is that we can bring out our inherent qualities of wisdom, courage, energy and compassion. We can transform our negative habits and tendencies ("karma", call it what you will) and show great proof of the power of this practice in the process. My practice helps me to feel clearer, more confident, more expansive and happier. It inspires me to respect my environment and be more considerate to other people. I guess it informs more or less everything about the way I conduct my daily life – even the way I drive my car! I have been doing it for half my life and, looking back, I can really see the changes it has made, not only to me but to everyone around me.'

What emerges from the above testimonies is that meditating, as conventionally understood in terms of a particular mental technique, is just the beginning of the process. Studying the teachings, encouraging and helping people, cultivating an 'attitude of gratitude', trying to maintain a calm and open disposition, being aware and sensitive without getting unduly swayed, are all aspects of Buddhism in daily life . . . Until one day we wake up and find that our daily life itself has become a meditation.

8

Buddhism in the world

Three poisons – and five onenesses

No fire like passion,
No jailer like hate,
No snare like delusion,
No torrent like craving.

How easy to see the faults of others –
We winnow them like chaff.
How hard to see one's own! –
We hide them, like cheating at dice.[36]

Buddhism's focus on the individual as the starting point for any change in society, its emphasis on pluralism and tolerance, and its image as monastic and detached, have led many commentators to see it as limited – even weak – in terms of political impact. Compared with the muscular histories of Christianity and Islam this certainly seems true. In the world of today, clamorous with slogans and lobby groups, it is hard to detect a loud Buddhist voice. Sometimes the lack of audibility is shocking.

Buddhists far outnumber Greens, for example, and yet are rarely interviewed about worldly affairs. Buddhism doesn't seem to lend itself to structural critique, institutional opposition or focused group protest.

There is no such thing as a 'Buddhist view' of economics or politics in the sense of a coherent, distinctive and program-matic set of 'solutions'. There is, however, a Buddhist analysis of the world situation. It is powerful, clear and remarkably straightforward. It derives from the teachings of the Five Precepts and Three Poisons. The five precepts are set out as follows:

THE FIVE PRECEPTS

1 Not to take life intentionally
2 Not to take what has not been given
3 Not to indulge in sexual misconduct
4 Not to speak falsely
5 Not to cloud the mind with intoxicants

The precepts are the nearest thing Buddhism has to the Christian commandments, though they are self-assumed and derived from rational principles rather than divine authority. They are expressed negatively, not in the stern sense of 'Thou shalt not . . .', but because articulating them in this way encourages Buddhists to explore the possibilities of what *is* recommended in any particular situation. 'Not to take what has not been given' means more than not to steal. You might, for example, find a purse in the street. You might not have stolen it; but neither does it belong to you. 'Not to speak falsely' means more than not to lie, for there is a big difference between telling part of the truth and telling the whole truth and nothing but the truth. And 'not to cloud the mind with intoxicants' is not necessarily the same as being teetotal. It might be pleasant and appropriate to share a glass of wine in certain circumstances, but that is very different from getting drunk. Buddhist teaching is rarely black and white. There is always a requirement on the practitioner to see the profound principle underlying the prescription and to use wisdom and compassion to interpret it according to circumstance and context.

The 'three poisons' which afflict humanity are greed, hatred and ignorance – or, as they are sometimes formulated, grasping, anger and delusion. The aim of Buddhism is to transform these negative states into their opposites, to turn the poisons into medicine. The emphasis, traditionally, has been on addressing these at an individual level, but they apply in the world with equal pertinence. Indeed, it is by seeing their operation on a vast scale that we can realize the full extent of the problem which faces us both as individuals and as global citizens.

Greed is at the root of the world's economic problems. The current epidemic of obesity in the richest countries is obvious evidence of this, but it goes much deeper. The guzzling of mineral resources and the hunger for more and newer material goods, are symptoms (and in turn causes) of the rampantly consumerist society in which we live. Productive work is commended in Buddhist teaching; but basing economic policy on a notion of 'growth' which is ultimately unsustainable flies in the face of the second precept.

Moreover, it would be one thing if we were *all* able to eat whatever we wanted whenever we wanted it, or own two cars, or jet to anywhere on the planet. But such options are only available to a tiny percentage of the world's population. The poison of greed therefore fuels inequity and suffering. And the attempt to capture, control and appropriate finite resources ushers in the greatest abomination of all – war.

There is no specifically Buddhist prescription for how to change the world economic system because Buddhism does not think in terms of systems. It is important, however, to remind ourselves that there was nothing inevitable about the growth of modern capitalism. It was not imposed. It evolved as a result of countless different individual choices. When the philosopher, Adam Smith, talked of an 'invisible hand' emerging as a result of these individual choices, he was making a point with which Buddhists would concur. The challenge for Buddhists is how to refocus those choices so that a new, better, more humane and more enlightened economics emerges. The world needs a wiser, fairer 'dominant ideology'.

After all, the presumed goal of getting and spending is not (just) profit: it is happiness. The Buddha showed this by his own personal example. He was born into a life of luxury, with rich friends, a wealthy family and all the material trappings anyone could wish for. Yet he gave all these up for the mendicant's bowl in order to find true joy and fulfilment.

In the tiny Himalayan kingdom of Bhutan they have a quotient called Gross National Happiness. When we, in the 'developed' world, have formulated similar indices and when the leaders of the G8 nations are genuinely competing with each other to help the poorer nations of the world, a new era of enlightened economics will have been born.

Meanwhile there are attempts by Buddhists all over the globe to engage[37] with these problems at a practical day-to-day level. To give just one example: the *Sarvodaya Shramadana* movement in Sri Lanka was founded by the activist and reformer Dr A. T. Ariyaratne. Sarvodaya means 'universal awakening' and Shramadana means 'sharing labour and energy'. Its origins go back to the 1950s when a group of school teachers from Colombo organized summer camps at which middle-class students gave up their vacations to work with the poor. Today about one third of Sri Lanka's villages have their own independent Sarvodaya societies and over 11,000 rural communities are actively engaged in Sarvodaya projects, including the construction of roads, irrigation canals, schools and other basic amenities. Drawing on Gandhi's ideal of *grama swaraj* or self-governing and self-sustaining village republics, individuals and groups are encouraged to form mutually supportive networks as a step towards the no-poverty, no-affluence society to which Ariyaratne aspires.

The underlying aim of the movement, as articulated in Ariyaratne's acceptance speech for the 1996 Gandhi Peace Prize, is a 'global transformation of human consciousness' designed to bring humanity closer to peace and justice. In his words, '*Metta* or loving kindness towards all sentient beings is the core spiritual consciousness which can transform global human relationships so that they are based on non-violence in thought, word and deed.'

The chief objective of Sarvodaya is . . . awakening. The root problem of poverty is . . . a sense of personal and collective powerlessness . . . 'Awakening' is to take place not in isolation but through social, economic, and political interaction. Personal awakening is seen as being interdependent with the awakening of one's local community, and both play a part in the awakening of one's nation and of the whole world.[38]

Greed is one of the prime causes of war. Enter the first precept and the second poison – hatred. Here again, to diagnose the problem is straightforward. Since time immemorial people have killed each other, torn apart families, ruined lives and livelihoods. There has been so much suffering. Mass killing has been justified in many ways. When World War One broke out there were plenty who spoke nobly of the sacrifices that were required. Was it worth it? There were many certainties at the time. From this distance it's not so clear.

But let's go straight to the hard question, the one that gets invoked to justify every conflict. What would Buddhists have done to stop Hitler? Or Stalin, Saddam, or any number of tyrants from history? Isn't killing them the only way?

A martial artist was once asked what he would do if a mad axe-man were charging towards him intent on attacking him. Would he try to reason with him, or run, or fight, or even kill his assailant in self-defence? The martial artist replied, ' I would try not to be there in the first place.'

To the anti-appeaser this is a glib and annoying cop-out. But it is also a profound answer because it challenges us to take responsibility for our situation. Who got us into this mess in the first place? What are we doing here? Are we part of the problem or the solution? Perhaps killing or neutralizing one very nasty individual does change the world. But the capture of Saddam hasn't stopped the violence in Iraq.

And what of the challenge posed by international terrorism as expressed in the recent atrocities? How do Buddhists respond?

First, they argue that we must, all of us, as individuals and as an international community, use every means at our disposal to understand and remedy the deep causes which have led to the current state of affairs. Lasting solutions cannot be found until we truly grasp the reasons why suffering arises. This may involve facing some awkward facts. Funding Osama Bin Laden and selling chemical weapons to Saddam Hussein, for example, were not wise policies. If we are not hypocrites, we must take responsibility for our own part in fuelling terrorism.

Second, we must respond to aggression without self-righteousness or hatred. We must engage in earnest and sincere dialogue with our perceived enemies, no matter how repugnant and misguided we feel their views to be. Only by demonstrating a better way forward and a more profound understanding of causation will we undermine their arguments. This is what it means to be truly strong.

Third, violence always leads to more violence, thereby causing a cycle of retaliation, which makes the chances of lasting peace even more remote. We must work hard to unlink this chain. Like the Buddha, who was forever seeking to communicate his teachings in the most effective way so as to meet the precise needs of the enquirer, we must exhaust all the resources at our disposal, employing 'skilful means' (*upaya*) and above all utilizing the power of 'hearts and minds' to break the cycle.

Finally, we must acknowledge that in any violent situation it is the weak, helpless, misguided and innocent who tend to suffer most, whoever the aggressor and whatever the cause may be. The generals and politicians survive to fight another day. The poor and hapless die. It is too easy – and getting ever easier – to kill and to send one's own troops to their death from a safe distance.

In the words of Daisaku Ikeda, 'Nothing is more barbarous than war, nothing more tragic.' Wars arise, in Buddhist terms, because a narrow, hardened and fundamentally deluded image of the 'Self' is projected outwards in such a way that all that is not 'me' or 'mine' is 'other', and to be regarded as alien and potentially threatening. The aim of Buddhist practice is to dissolve this sharp boundary-line until egocentric preoccupations subside and are replaced by a greater appreciation of the interconnectedness and interdependence of all beings.

This is not to say that Buddhists have never been involved in wars. Some of the worst horrors of the twentieth century occurred in South-East Asia. Buddhists have certainly engaged in military and nationalistic conflict, some even invoking religion as a justification. However, there is no explicit doctrine of a 'just war' in Buddhism, and those who advocate violent action do so in flagrant disregard of the key virtue of 'non-violence' (*ahimsa*) and the pacifist teachings of the scriptures. Nor is there any equivalent in Buddhist history to the blood shed in the name of the great monotheistic religions: no crusade, no inquisition and no holocaust.

There are countless Buddhist groups (and groups which include Buddhists) in the world today working for peace and social justice.[39] One of the most notable of these is the Buddhist Peace Fellowship in America, which has a membership of thousands and works assiduously with two prominent activist programmes: the Buddhist Alliance for Social Engagement (BASE) and the International Network of Engaged Buddhists (INEB). Will their efforts and those of countless individuals around the planet achieve anything in the face of the massed ranks of the arms trade? It is a very difficult challenge, especially in a world where the prime minister of the United Kingdom seems keener to shake the hand of Colonel Gadaffi than to meet the Dalai Lama.

Tibet, the homeland of the Dalai Lama, is an interesting case. Should the Tibetans have taken up arms? Thousands have perished there since the Chinese occupation in 1950. On the other hand, countless Buddhists have spread across the world as a result of the persecution, bringing the teachings with them, spreading the message of peace and, creating value, whereas perhaps nearly as many innocent civilians were killed in Iraq by the 'Forces of Liberation' as by the Saddam regime. Misguided actions lead to unintended consequences.

Buddhism seeks to help us act wisely, compassionately and appropriately in every situation. Sometimes this means intervening immediately, sometimes it means stepping back and taking a longer view. 'But in the long run we are all dead,' protest the 'pragmatists'. Exactly. In the words of a Buddhist sage, 'Life as a human being is hard to sustain – as hard as it is for the dew to remain on the grass. But it is better to live a single day with honour than to live to the age of 120 and die in disgrace.'[40]

Finally – ignorance. This is the hardest poison of the three for us to see in ourselves. Indeed it presents a philosophical conundrum, for we may to be too ignorant and deluded to realize how ignorant and deluded we are. Ignorance underpins all injustice and oppression because it refuses to see the essential equality and dignity of every human being. It fosters racial bigotry and cultural sectarianism because it cannot delight in difference. It stifles compassion and refuses to engage in openhearted dialogue. It disrespects human rights and has no environmental awareness. It fuels the drive for short-term gratification rather than longer-term collective benefit, the pursuit of ends over means, arrogance about our position in the world or in history, contempt for that of others. Ignorance is blind to the fundamental ecology of existence.

A medieval Chinese scholar, Miao-Lo, developed a schema called the Ten Onenesses. Its premise is the essential connectedness of life, a principle expressed as 'Two but not Two'. The idea is that, when deluded, we tend to see the differences between things rather than what links them. We observe two distinct phenomena and fail to realize the extent to which they are related. Five of the Onenesses are technical, specific, and difficult to explain briefly; but the other five have become common features of any holistic analysis.

FIVE OF THE TEN ONENESSES[41]

1   Oneness of body and mind
2   Oneness of internal and external
3   Oneness of cause and effect
4   Oneness of life and its environment
5   Oneness of thought, word and deed

Buddhism rejects 'dualism'. Only by developing our consciousness of the profound connection between the causes we make and the effects we see in the world around us will we understand how best to live. We have to transform our greed, hatred and ignorance into generosity, compassion and wisdom. A new alchemy is needed. We must turn the poisons into medicine.

9

Buddhism in the twenty-first century

Is the future orange?

The religion of the future will be a cosmic religion. It should transcend personal God and avoid dogma and theology. Covering both the natural and the spiritual, it should be based on a religious sense arising from the experience of all things natural and spiritual as a meaningful unity. Buddhism answers this description ... If there is any religion that could cope with modern scientific needs it would be Buddhism.[42]

Was Einstein right? How will Buddhism develop in the twenty-first century? Prediction can be a dangerous exercise. Who could have foreseen that the Chinese army's invasion of a poor, mountain-locked country would make a monk in a maroon robe one of the most famous people in the world? Who might have imagined that the word 'karma' would be bandied around today as part of everyday speech? Or that there would be a Peace Pagoda in Battersea Park, London, or a cult novel and movie called *The Buddha of Suburbia* or a fifteen-acre Taiwanese Buddhist temple site in Los Angeles? ...

Buddhism has proved remarkably resilient and adaptive so far. Time will tell whether it can respond to the challenges of the coming century and continue as a vibrant, living, relevant tradition.

Will it still thrive in South-East Asia, where for so long it has been part of an essentially rural way of life, as that region becomes ever more industrialized? Will it make any impression on the Muslim world? So far its impact there has been minimal: its pluralistic tendencies don't seem to chime naturally with the needs and aspirations of Islamic societies. But there are the beginnings of dialogue and there *is* common ground for those who are prepared to chart it.

China presents an interesting challenge for crystal-ball gazers. Will the Buddhism which was suppressed at the time of the Cultural Revolution reassert itself as the religion of the world's next superpower?

As to Africa, who can say what will happen in that troubled continent? One eminent Buddhist leader has called this 'The Century of Africa', so maybe many of the answers about our future lie there. Certainly there can be no lasting or just peace in the world while so many of its citizens suffer in such abject poverty.

And what of the West, with its vast wealth and control of so many of the world's material resources? Will it maintain or even increase its hegemony? A recent survey estimated that by 2015 half the people on the planet will speak English, so what happens to Buddhism in the Anglophone countries will be very important.

When I put some of these questions about the future development of Buddhism to a friend of mine she responded instantly: 'Buddhism has never been more relevant or important. It is about empowering the individual. We've all got to take individual responsibility for changing ourselves and changing the world.'

There seems to be some truth in this assessment. Making sense of change lies at the heart of Buddhism, and rapid change is the most pronounced feature of modern living. It is no good any longer relying on a job for life, or a guaranteed pension scheme, or colleagues from the office, school – or even the family. Nor can we look to the state for sustenance. The era of nationalized industries and centralized welfare schemes appears to have passed. We live in an ever more atomized society. We are all individuals now. We must each strive diligently to work out our own path. And we must try to support each other in that process.

It is certain that science and technology will play an ever-increasing part in our lives as this century progresses. Buddhists need have no inherent fear of this. Long before Copernicus was condemned for daring to suggest that the earth was not the centre of the universe, Buddhist scriptures described a multiplicity of galaxies and solar systems of which this planet was just one tiny part. Heisenberg's revolutionary Principle of Uncertainty, from which chaos theory grew, came as no shocking revelation to Buddhists, who had always appreciated the indivisibility of subject and object, self and environment.

When the internet came along it was rapidly and confidently embraced by those with access to a computer. Buddhist email discussion forums proliferated as a means of exchanging ideas, encouragement and inspiration. Electronic archives (the first was established at the Australian National University in 1992) were set up to hold a variety of Buddhist resources – copies of original documents, bibliographies, directories, texts, poetry and other materials. With the advent of Unicode, texts in their original languages could be consulted online, along with electronic dictionaries to help decipher them. In 1993 the online *Journal of Buddhist Ethics* began publication. Today it has more than 6,000 subscribers in over fifty countries worldwide. At last the possibility of a 'CyberSangha' exists, a global online Buddhist community transcending time and place, geography and culture. Perhaps the technological future is indeed orange?

What of the moral and ethical challenges prompted by the ever-quickening pace of scientific and technological development? Two in particular seem set to present pressing new dilemmas: genetic engineering and euthanasia. They go to the very heart of what it is to be human – the beginnings and ends of human life and human identity.

Buddhism's view of procreation is very different from that described by the monotheistic religions. Sexual reproduction has no divinely sanctioned priority over alternative modes of procreation. There is, therefore, no reason in principle why reproductive cloning should not be seen as just another way of creating life, neither intrinsically better nor worse than any other. Therapeutic cloning does, however, pose a problem, for it involves the destruction of embryonic life; and life as a human, according to Buddhist teachings, begins at the moment of conception. Ending an unborn life is, therefore, equal in gravity to taking the life of someone already born – in theory at least. In practice, the potential benefits from genetic engineering in terms of the reduction of suffering are plain for all to see and some Buddhists would argue in its favour on overriding grounds of compassion.[43]

Equivalent ethical dilemmas can be identified in the discussion surrounding euthanasia. Advocates stress the compassionate motivation of reducing suffering and opponents invoke the first precept. It may be possible to argue for a difference between 'active' euthanasia (the deliberate killing of a patient, by lethal injection for example) and 'passive' euthanasia (not providing life support), though this seems casuistic if the intention is the same and the outcome is beyond doubt. And it will become an increasingly difficult distinction to make as ever more sophisticated interventions are devised to prolong life.

What the debates about genetic engineering and euthanasia presage is a growing discussion about, on the one hand, the roles, responsibilities and rights of the family, the state and the medical authorities and, on the other, the autonomy and authority of the individual, the nature of free will and the value of life itself. The arguments have been rehearsed volubly. The debate seems set to intensify with every new medical advance.

Where Buddhism may be able to make a valuable and distinctive contribution is in reminding the participants of the dangers of moralizing or being too dogmatic. Buddhism does not assert a moral obligation to preserve life at all costs. Recognizing – and indeed using – the inevitability of death is a central tenet of its teachings. Death cannot be postponed for ever, and Buddhists are encouraged to be mindful and properly prepared to embrace it when the hour duly comes. To seek to prolong life for the sake of it by recourse to ever more elaborate technology is a denial of the reality of human mortality and, in certain circumstances, a manifestation of delusion (*moha*) and excessive attachment (*trishna*).

An unwillingness to face up to the inevitability of death may be emerging as one of the most obvious indications of where Western society is deluded. For all the fantastical life-extending discoveries produced in modern medical laboratories, we don't appear to be very good as a culture at dealing with the ageing process. We accord old people less importance and respect than earlier generations. And we seem to find talking about death more difficult than our Victorian predecessors, for all that we mock their sexual hang-ups. Coming to terms with mortality is a sign of maturity and it may prove to be one of Buddhism's finest contributions to the living now and the living to come.

> Death is neither depressing nor exciting; it is simply a fact of life.
>
> Sogyal Rinpoche

> On the day that you were born, you began to die. Do not waste a single moment more!
>
> Dilgo Khyentse Rinpoche

> Letting go is a central theme in spiritual practice as we see the preciousness and brevity of life.
>
> Jack Kornfield

A fourth turn of the wheel?

Buddhism teaches that past, present and future are inseparable. If we want to understand what is happening today, we need to look at what we did yesterday; and if we look at what we are doing today we can get a better sense of what will happen tomorrow.

Sadly, by that yardstick, war, poverty, injustice and environmental degradation will be with us for many tomorrows to come. But Buddhism is well-equipped philosophically and morally to face the challenges of the future. It has never been 'fixed' or dogmatically unitary. It can embrace modernity, relativism and contingency. It understands relationship.

As traditional structures decay new ones take their place, webs and linkages and networks, new ways of organizing ourselves and communicating with each other, mostly driven by rapid advances in computer technology. Were the Buddha to visit London or New York today he might be shocked to discover that its citizens seem to know hardly any of their neighbours. But he might be equally struck by the fact that so many of them spend so much time on the phone to friends many miles and hours away.

For although we are atomized, and possibly even alienated from older community structures and allegiances, we are, as never before, citizens of the world. Whether we like it or not, we can no longer pretend we are separate. We are all connected. We live in a global village. A philosophy that can embrace this truth is what is needed. A philosophy that transcends national, regional, ethnic, racial, cultural (and religious) differences. A global philosophy.

In terms of attitudes to sex and gender, Buddhism has a better start than many of the other major religions. Buddhist cultures have tended not to be as exercised about sexual and gender taboos as, for example, Christian or Islamic ones. Homosexuality is not condoned; but neither is it persecuted. Using contraception does not present ideological problems. Women were ordained from the outset, and although there are traditional forms of Buddhism which are blatantly patriarchal and male-centred, the barriers to women do not seem as high as in many other religions.[44]

In terms of race and ethnicity, Buddhism has not been as successful as either Islam or Christianity in attracting black converts in the West – so far at least. Perhaps this is because of less aggressive proselytizing, for there is no inherent problem in crossing cultures and embracing diversity. There is no requirement to rest from work on the Sabbath, or dress in a certain way. Nor are there any special dietary rules (many Buddhists are vegetarian but not all) or hygiene codes. Buddhism is nothing if not adaptable and pluralistic. It has never been a 'one-party' state.[45]

In terms of wealth and class, there are few intrinsic financial or status barriers. The materials with which the practice is traditionally associated (incense, beads, candles and so on) are not costly. There is no membership fee. Tithes are not required. There is great emphasis on the importance of contribution, including financial donation, but nothing in the scriptures which enjoins Buddhists (apart from those in a monastic context) to adopt a particular attitude towards wealth, other than that it should be earned honestly and via a job that does not involve causing suffering. As to the disparity of resources and power in the world, Buddhism can be used to justify both quietist, social conservatism and radical redistribution along the lines of liberation theology. There is no clear-cut, out-and-out Buddhist prescription other than an emphasis on non-violent change.

One aspect of Buddhism does seem to present an obstacle for a number of practitioners, especially in the West, namely the importance given to the role of the teacher or mentor. In Asia, religious teachers are rarely challenged and their interpretation of the teachings is often accepted uncritically by their followers. Since the teacher is often also the head or director of the school or sect, unilateral decisions may be taken concerning the management of the organization. It is an approach which tends to put off more people in the West than it attracts. Here, Dharma centres have preferred to adopt constitutions and procedures which are more transparent and consultative. Rather than concentrating power in a single pair of hands, they tend to channel authority through a committee structure with delegated responsibility for areas such as finance and public relations. The role of the mentor is thus confined to giving spiritual leadership and pastoral guidance.

It is very difficult to imagine that the monastic tradition within Buddhism, one of its most distinctive contributions to the world, won't decline under the pressures of the modern world. It has in every other culture. The tension between withdrawal from the bustling world and whole-hearted engagement in it seems more difficult than ever to sustain. But not impossible. And definitely necessary, for there will have to be a concerted challenge of some sort to rampant consumerism if we are to survive as a species. What the blue planet needs now, as never before, is a 'culture of awakening'.[46]

Buddhists, especially from traditional backgrounds, also face the challenge and opportunity of meeting each other, perhaps for the first time, and discovering that there are other forms of Buddhism from the ones they are used to, with different emphases and interpretations. Fifty years ago there were virtually no Buddhists in London or New York. Now more or less every variety of Buddhist expression in the world is to be found in Bloomsbury or Manhattan. The marketplace for belief has never presented such a bewildering array of choice. Perhaps we can look forward to a new era of Buddhist ecumenism.

Where will the next generation of Buddhists come from? Four groups:

First, the children of those who practise already and continue to find relevance, utility and attraction in its teachings.

Second, people disillusioned with other religions. Many Christians and Jews, for example, value formal religious expression, ritual and regular practice, but feel unhappy about the guilt which their traditions seem to induce. Buddhism has no concept of guilt and, of course, no overweening God figure, which makes it very attractive.

Third, people journeying from one of the newer forms of religious expression and New Age philosophies. They will already be familiar with some Buddhist concepts, because many of its principles have already been absorbed or incorporated, albeit in a diluted form. It is still hard to find anyone who actively dislikes what (they think) Buddhism stands for, though there is a suspicion of anything that smacks too much of 'organized religion'.

Fourth, people of no religion, who are attracted by Buddhism's pragmatic humanism, its ethics, and perhaps, its psychotherapeutic insights. Buddhism could well be seen as the most elaborated form of Depth Psychology yet devised. Jung was certainly influenced by it. To be truly modern, he argued, we must be 'conscious to a superlative degree'. To be fully developed 'requires the most intensive and extensive consciousness, with a minimum of unconsciousness . . . He alone is fully conscious who is conscious of the present.'[47]

So, might we be on the verge of a fourth turning of the wheel of the Dharma? Are we witnessing the dawn of a new 'Axial Age'? Only time will tell. And maybe that's not the whole point anyway. The Buddha wasn't interested in forming a religion. He emphatically told people he was not superhuman. He had no desire to be made into a deity. He chose not to appoint a successor because he was suspicious of organized hierarchy. He may not even have wanted to have followers. The teachings were what counted. Like a good doctor his deepest wish would have been to be unnecessary. What he wanted more than anything else was to help people work it out for themselves.

Notes

1 My colloquial rendition. For an account of the full exchange between Buddha and Malunkyaputta, see Walpola Rahula, *What the Buddha Taught*, pp.13–15.

2 *Majjhima Nikaya* 1.265, quoted in Michael Carrithers, *The Buddha*, p. 4.

3 *Writings of Nichiren Daishonin*, p. 851.

4 The metaphor is a common one: the precise words are those of the Japanese sage, Nichiren (*Writings of Nichiren Daishonin*, p. 125).

5 After Christianity, Islam and Hinduism. For more about whether or not Buddhism constitutes a 'religion' in the formal sense of the term, see Damien Keown, *Buddhism: A Very Short Introduction*, pp. 3–15.

6 See *http://en.wikipedia.org/wiki/Buddhism_by_country*

7 Jinananda, *Warrior of Peace*, p. 59.

8 Ashvaghosha, *Buddhacarita*, 5.18–19 quoted in Jinananda, *Warrior of Peace*, pp. 26–27.

9 *Majjhima Nikaya*, 1, 245 quoted in Carrithers, *The Buddha*, pp. 47–48. This vividly self-aware account is, of course, a 'reported' version of the Buddha's story, written down centuries after he had died.

10 *Jataka Nidana (The Story of Gotama Buddha)*, p. 99. For a clearer, less compressed account, see Sutra 36 of the *Majjhima Nikaya*: http://www.accesstoinsight.org/canon/sutta/majjhima/mn-036x-tb0.html

11 Daisaku Ikeda, *The Living Buddha*, p. 68.

12 Yasuji Kiimura (Ed.), *Outline of Buddhism*, NSIC, Japan, 1981, pp. 16–17.

13 Quoted in Rahula Walpola, *What the Buddha Taught*, pp. 127, 128, 132.

14 Pillar Edict 2.

15 To give but five:

'No construction lasts forever. So keep your minds on it. Make it happen.' Richard Gombrich (unpublished MS).

'All conditioned things are liable to decay. With mindfulness strive.' Jinananda, *Warrior of Peace*, p. 123.

'Transient are conditioned things. Try to accomplish your aim with diligence.' Rahula Walpola, *What the Buddha Taught*, p. 138.

'All individual things pass away. Seek your liberation with diligence.' Karen Armstrong, *Buddha*, p. 171.

'Everything that is born is subject to decay. Since there is no external saviour it is up to each of you to work out your own liberation.' Hope and Van Loon, *Introducing Buddha*, p. 45.

16 Fritjof Capra explores this wonderfully in his classic *The Tao of Physics: An Exploration of the Parallels between Modern Physics and Eastern Mysticism*.

17 For a discussion of Atman, Brahman, traditional Vedic belief and the historical and philosophical context within which the Buddha framed his analysis see Richard Gombrich, *How Buddhism Began*.

18 Elizabeth J. Harris, *What Buddhists Believe*, p. 38.

19 And, as Douglas Adams reminds us, whether or not we will be able to find a parking space when we get there.

20 Rebirth and reincarnation are not strictly speaking the same. Reincarnation suggests the same entity taking human form, whereas rebirth could take a number of different forms – as set out in what follows.

21 Charles S. Prebish and Damien Keown, *Buddhism: The eBook*, p. 44.

22 See Richard Causton, *The Buddha in Daily Life*, chapter 1.

23 For an example of the former, see the recent writings of Stephen Batchelor; for the latter, see those of Richard Gombrich.

24 Windhorse Publications, Birmingham, 2004.

25 The simplest formulation of this is as follows: 'When this exists, that comes to be. With the arising of this, that arises. When this does not exist, that does not come to be. With the cessation of this, that ceases.' *Majjhima Nikaya* 2.32.

26 In early Buddhism this analysis is formalized into what is known as The Twelvefold Law of Causation. In reverse order: (12) Ageing and dying are conditioned by birth, for without birth there would be no death; (11) Birth is conditioned by becoming; (10) Becoming is conditioned by attachment; (9) Attachment is conditioned by craving; (8) Craving is conditioned by sensation;(7) Sensation is conditioned by contact; (6) Contact is conditioned by the six sense organs; (5) The six sense organs are conditioned by mind and body; (4) Mind and body are conditioned by consciousness; (3) Consciousness is conditioned by karma; (2) Karma is conditioned by ignorance. Thus, according to this formulation, ignorance is the ultimate link in the chain, the source from which all existence and suffering arise. See Walpola Rahula, *What the Buddha Taught*, pp. 53–54.

27 From *The Middle-Length Discourses of the Buddha*, quoted in Elizabeth J. Harris and Ramona Kauth (Eds.), *Meeting Buddhists*, p. 287.

28 The form of words used as a formal expression of commitment to Buddhism's three 'jewels'.

29 Ringu Tulku, a Tibetan Buddhist monk, quoted in Elizabeth J. Harris, *What Buddhists Believe*, p. 54.

30 Verses from the *Dhammapada*, quoted in Elizabeth J. Harris and Ramona Kauth (Eds.), *Meeting Buddhists*, p. 288.

31 My paraphrase, see *Writings of Nichiren Daishonin*, p. 3.

32 I should qualify this: 'most Buddhists in the West'. Many Asian Buddhists, and possibly the majority, concentrate on earning 'merit' through creating 'good karma'. But action, as becomes clearer later in this chapter, is indivisible from meditation if it is right-minded.

33 The sentiments are Buddhist; the words are those of Pliny the Elder.

34 See http://www.dailycardinal.com/news/2005/02/01/Science/Meditation.Provides.longTerm.Benefits-847382.shtml and http://www.meaningoflife.i12.com/meditation-article.htm

35 Peter J. Conradi, *Going Buddhist*, has a lovely chapter on meditating. See also, Jim Pym, *You Don't Have to Sit on the Floor*.

36 Verses from the *Dhammapada*, quoted in Elizabeth J. Harris and Ramona Kauth (Eds.), *Meeting Buddhists*, p. 291.

37 The Vietnamese monk, Thich Nhat Hanh, is the best known pioneer of so-called 'Engaged Buddhism'. It could be argued that the need to found such a movement implies a perceived danger of 'dis-engagement'.

38 The full text is quoted on the Sarvodaya USA website: http://phoenix.akasha.de/~sarvdaya/sarvodayaphilos.html

39 See Elizabeth J. Harris, *What Buddhists Believe*, chapter 5, for a catalogue of inspiring and courageous examples of such activity.

40 *Writings of Nichiren Daishonin*, p. 871.

41 The other five are: The oneness of the goal of practice and the true nature of phenomena; the oneness of the impure and pure; the oneness of self and others; the oneness of the provisional and true teachings; the oneness of benefit.

42 Albert Einstein, quoted in Lama Surya Das, *Awakening the Buddha Within*, p. xv.

43 For a discussion of the parallel debate about abortion, see Damien Keown, *VSI Buddhist Ethics*, Chapter 6.

44 I don't wish to appear smug about this, especially as a Western male. See Elizabeth J. Harris, *What Buddhists Believe*, chapter 5, for a fuller treatment of the position of women in Buddhism.

45 Peter Harvey, *An Introduction to Buddhism*, p. 4.

46 Stephen Batchelor, *Buddhism without Beliefs*, pp. 109–115.

47 C. G. Jung, 'The Spiritual Problem of Modern Man', in *Modern Man in Search of a Soul*, p. 227.

References

Armstrong, Karen, *Buddha*, London, Phoenix, 2000

Batchelor, Stephen, *Buddhism Without Beliefs*, London, Bloomsbury, 1997

Capra, Fritjof, *The Tao of Physics*, London, Flamingo, 1989

Conradi, Peter J., *Going Buddhist*, London, Short Books, 2004

Carrithers, Michael, *Buddha* (Past Masters Series), Oxford, OUP, 1983

Causton, Richard, *The Buddha in Daily Life*, London, Rider, 1995

Das, Lama Surya, *Awakening the Buddha Within*, London, Bantam, 1997

Follmi, Danielle and Olivier, *Buddhist Offerings 365 Days*, London, Thames & Hudson, 2003

Gombrich, Richard, *Theravada Buddhism*, London, Routledge, 2005

Gombrich, Richard, *How Buddhism Began*, London, Routledge, 2005

Gombrich, Richard, *The Buddha: A Historical Biography*, unpublished manuscript

Harris, Elizabeth J., *What Buddhists Believe*, Oxford, Oneworld, 1998

Harris, Elizabeth J. and Kauth, Ramona (Eds.), *Meeting Buddhists*, Leicester, Christians Aware, 2005

Harvey, Peter, *An Introduction to Buddhism*, Cambridge, CUP, 1990

Hope, Jane and Van Loon, Borin, *Introducing Buddha*, New York, Totem, 1995

Ikeda, Daisaku, *The Living Buddha*, New York, Weatherhill, 1976

Jinananda, *Warrior of Peace: The Life of the Buddha*, Birmingham, Windhorse, 2002

Jung, C. G., *Modern Man in Search of a Soul*, London, Ark, 1984

Keown, Damien, *A Dictionary of Buddhism*, Oxford, OUP, 2003

Keown, Damien, *Buddhism: A Very Short Introduction*, Oxford, OUP, 1996

Keown, Damien, *Buddhist Ethics: A Very Short Introduction*, Oxford, OUP, 2005

Kiimura, Yasuji (Ed.), *Outline of Buddhism*, Tokyo, NSIC, 1981

Nagapriya, *Exploring Karma and Rebirth*, Birmingham, Windhorse, 2004

Nichiren, *The Writings of Nichiren Daishonin*, Tokyo, Soka Gakkai, 1999

Pali Text Society, *The Story of Gotama Buddha (Jataka-Nidana)*, trans. N. A. Jayawickrama, Oxford, Pali Text Society, 1990

Prebish, Charles S. and Keown, Damien, *Buddhism: The eBook*, London, Online Books, 2004

Rahula, Walpola Sri, *What the Buddha Taught*, Oxford, Oneworld, 1997

Further reading

There are a number of more detailed introductions to Buddhism. These include:

Gethin, Rupert, *The Foundations of Buddhism*, Oxford, OUP, 1998

Harvey, Peter., *An Introduction to Buddhism: Teachings, History, and Practices*, Cambridge, CUP, 1990

Mitchell, D. W., *Buddhism: Introducing the Buddhist Experience*, New York and Oxford, OUP, 2002

Robinson, R. H., Johnson, W. L., Wawrytko, S. A. and DeGraff, G., *The Buddhist Religion: A Historical Introduction*, Belmont CA, Wadsworth, 1996

There is an excellent guide to further reading, key resources and places to visit in Elizabeth J. Harris and Ramona Kauth (Eds.), *Meeting Buddhists*, Leicester, Christians Aware, 2005

Websites

There are innumerable websites devoted to all aspects of Buddhism: a recent Google search for 'Buddhism' returned over two million hits! All the main groups and schools have web pages. In addition there are many academic and personal sites, most of which contain links to other sites of interest. Websites come and go, but three which have stood the test of time are:

Dharmanet (www.dharmanet.org), a gateway to a range of Buddhist resources providing a comprehensive listing of groups and publications, including 'Socially Engaged Buddhism Resources'.

Access to Insight (www.accesstoinsight.org), a comprehensive range of resources on Theravada teachings.

The Journal of Buddhist Ethics (www.gold.ac.uk), which publishes academic articles on ethical issues, and also has a global resources page.

In addition, I recommend consulting the information posted by Peter Harvey on the website of the *UK Association for Buddhist Studies* (UKABS) as part of the Sunderland University MA course in Buddhist studies: (http://www.sunderland.ac.uk/~os0dwe/bs6.html)

Contacts

UK and Europe

A useful guide to Buddhist groups in the UK is the *Buddhist Directory*, published by the Buddhist Society (www.thebuddhistsociety.org). The ninth edition is now available and lists over 500 Buddhist places around the United Kingdom. The guide is indexed by centre name, location and tradition, and has a new section on the centres offering retreat facilities.

Also available and extending its coverage beyond the UK is *The Buddhist Directory: A Unique Reference to Europe's and the Rest of the World's Buddhist Centres* by Peter Lorie and Julie Foakes (Gill and Macmillan, 1996).

An online guide is provided by *BuddhaNet* at www.buddhanet.net/euro_dir/eur_ukil.htm. See also www.nbo.org.uk

USA and Canada

A comprehensive guide to Buddhist centres in the USA and Canada can be found in the *Complete Guide to Buddhist America* by Don Morreale. Published by Shambhala, it lists over a thousand meditation centres.

Index and Glossary